Lernkrimi American English

Murderous Network

Gina Billy
Timothy Woods Palma

compact

Weitere Informationen zu Compact Lernkrimis finden Sie am Ende des Buches und unter www.lernkrimi.de.

Chefredaktion: Dr. Matthias Feldbaum
Redaktion: Marie Frey
Fachkorrektur: Rosemarie Correia
Produktion: Frank Speicher
Titelillustration: Karl Knospe
Lernkrimi-Logo: Carsten Abelbeck
Umschlaggestaltung: EKH Werbeagentur GbR
Typografischer Entwurf: EKH Werbeagentur GbR, Hartmut Baier

ISBN 978-3-8174-9312-8
381749312/1

www.compactverlag.de, www.lernkrimi.de

Vorwort

Liebe Leserin, lieber Leser,
sicher zum Lernerfolg – mit Spaß und Spannung! Die Compact Lernkrimis mit ihrer Kombination aus Lektüre und didaktischem Übungsanteil eignen sich hervorragend, um breite Sprachkompetenzen in der Fremdsprache zu erwerben. Der Lerner wird dabei durch die spannende Handlung, das angemessene Sprachniveau und den stetig ansteigenden Schwierigkeitsgrad der Übungen gefördert und motiviert.
Entwickelt nach neuesten Erkenntnissen der Fremdsprachendidaktik, sind Compact Lernkrimis das ideale Medium für einen Lernerfolg im Selbststudium. Durch die kleinen Texteinheiten und den hohen Übungsanteil sind sie aber auch als Unterrichtslektüre bestens geeignet.

So lernen Sie mit Compact Lernkrimis:

- **Mit Begeisterung lernen:** Die packende Krimihandlung motiviert Sie beim Lesen des englischen Originaltextes.
- **Wissen intensivieren und erweitern:** Durch die Kombination aus didaktisierter Lektüre und textbezogenen Übungen testen und trainieren Sie Ihre Sprachkenntnisse effektiv. Vokabelangaben auf jeder Seite unterstützen Sie beim Lesen.
- **Systematisch lernen:** Knüpfen Sie an Ihr individuelles Sprachniveau an und setzen Sie eigene Lernziele – linear im Schwierigkeitsgrad ansteigend oder mit punktuellen Schwerpunkten von Grundwortschatz bis Hörverstehen.
- **Unabhängig sein:** Lernen Sie ganz individuell – wo und wann Sie wollen.

Viel Spaß beim **spannend Englisch lernen**
wünscht Ihnen

Prof. Dr. Christiane Neveling
Didaktik der romanischen Sprachen, Universität Leipzig

Inhalt

Murderous Network

Gina Billy

1 Neighborhood Network

Miguel Alvarado opened the front door of his family farmhouse in Sunnyvale, California and stepped outside. He stretched his tired, 57-year-old body as he looked at the beautiful land in front of him. The first light of the morning was shining on a row of cherry trees. They separated the small house from Miguel's five acres of strawberry fields. The trees were the only ones left from what used to be a huge orchard. Miguel remembered the day his father had planted the fruit trees over 40 years ago. That was just a few years before the Santa Clara Valley got its new name. When Miguel was a boy, the southern part of the San Francisco Bay Area was still known as "The Valley of Heart's Delight[i]." But since the early 1980s, the whole world called it Silicon Valley. Miguel's little urban farm was one of only a handful left in Sunnyvale. Most of the other landowners had cashed out, including the Green family who used to own the land on both sides of Miguel's place.

> **The Valley of Heart's Delight** ist eine andere Bezeichnung für **Silicon Valley,** das das Santa Clara Valley und einen Teil von San Francisco umfasst. Silicon Valley (silicon = Silizium) ist heute einer der wichtigsten Standorte der Computertechnologie und High-Tech-Industrie.

Miguel got angry when he thought about what the computer and high-tech industry had done to the landscape. His dark brown eyes looked to the west. He saw the big, old ranch house that belonged to his neighbor and friend, Nathan Green. Nathan's father, Ethan, had sold most of the 500 acres of his ranch lands to property investors in the late 70s and made a fortune. Miguel then looked to the east and stared at the huge building next to his property. It was the headquarters of Martin-Woods Network Systems. Miguel didn't know – or care about – exactly what work the company did. He only knew that MWNS, Inc. was involved in the computer industry. It belonged to a woman he hated with all his heart, Sophie Martin-Woods. She was responsible for the construction of the new main building. It was so big and tall that the shadow from its glass walls kept his strawberries in the shade for most of the morning. That reminded Miguel that it was time to start the long work day. Impatiently, he went back into the house to call his children. "Jose? Carmelita? Get moving! The first pick-your-own customers will be here soon!"

acre	Hektar
orchard	Obstplantage
delight	Entzücken
urban farm	städtischer Bauernhof
to cash out	Vermögen verkaufen
headquarters	Firmenhauptsitz
shade	Schatten
pick-your-own	Selbstpflück-

The sleepy voice of Miguel's 17-year-old son answered from the kitchen. "Oh, Dad, come on, it's Saturday! And by the way, when are you going to start calling me Joe like everyone else does?"
"Never, Jose! Now, where's your sister?"
"Carmelita is already outside. Rosa's not feeling well, so Carmelita is feeding the chickens and Hera."
Hera was Carmelita's dog, a six-month-old Labrador Retriever.
"What's wrong with your mom? Has she got a headache again?"
"Rosa is NOT my mother! She's my stepmother," Joe said angrily. "Carmelita's too," he added, more calmly. He didn't want to think about his mom right now. It hurt too much.

Exercise 1: Choose the right word. **Lesen Sie weiter und unterstreichen Sie das richtige Wort!**

Joe also didn't **1.** like / want to have another **2.** fight / argue with his dad, especially today. He was planning to **3.** ask / question his father if he could stop **4.** job / work earlier than usual. He had tons of **5.** housework / homework to do for school and wanted to go to a study group at a friend's house.

Lisa was going to be there. She was Sophie Martin-Woods's pretty, 16-year-old daughter. Even though they were still "just friends", lately they had started flirting with each other a little bit. But their parents couldn't know about that!

"Dad! Joe! Come quickly! Something terrible has happened!" 14-year-old Carmelita ran into the house. Her beautiful eyes were filled with tears, and her face was white with shock. What worried Miguel the most, though, was his daughter's hands. They were covered in blood!

"Sweetheart, what's wrong? Have you hurt yourself?" Miguel asked and put an arm around her shaking shoulders.

"No, it's Hera – and the marigolds you planted around the strawberry fields. Oh Daddy, I… I can't say it! Just come with me!"

tons of	jede Menge
marigold	Ringelblume
to curse	fluchen
organic farming	biologische Landwirtschaft
Madre de Dios (*Spanish*)	Mutter Gottes

Carmelita used one of her hands to try to wipe away the tears, and this left bloody streaks on her face. Without another word, she turned and ran back outside. Her dad and brother ran behind her through the cherry trees and out to the fields. When they arrived, the sight in front of them made Miguel fall to his knees and begin cursing in Spanish. Yesterday, hundreds of yellow and orange marigolds had surrounded his fields of bright red berries. The flowers were part of Miguel's organic farming[i] methods. Marigolds kept certain harmful insects and dust away from the fruit. But his marigolds wouldn't be doing that anymore. Someone had pulled each and every flower out of the ground and broken the plants in half. It was an act of cruel vandalism, and it would cost Miguel a lot of time and money to re-plant with mature flowers. But why hadn't Hera warned them? Even though she was so young, Hera was already a great watch dog. Then he remembered what else Carmelita had said – and the blood on her hands. "Madre de Dios," he whispered.

Organic farming (ökologische Landwirtschaft, Ökolandbau) ist eine Form der Landwirtschaft, die unter anderem auf chemische Düngung und Gentechnik verzichtet. Die Nachfrage nach „Bio-Produkten" wächst weltweit stetig.

Exercise 2: Prepositions. Lesen Sie weiter und setzen Sie die richtigen Präpositionen ein!

In on of over off away

Miguel took his eyes **1.** off the dead flowers and saw his children a short distance **2.** away.

They were both crying now and **kneeling** 3. in the middle of the first field. Miguel stepped 4. ~~over~~ on several berries as he went 5. over to join them. Even though Miguel was expecting it, the sight 6. of Hera's lifeless body also brought tears to his own eyes.

Someone had cut the poor dog's throat, and there was blood all over the place. The knife was still stuck in Hera's body. A piece of paper with flecks of blood on it was taped to it. Miguel started to reach for the paper.

"No, Dad! Don't touch anything," Joe warned. "The police will need to take photographs and see everything just the way it is."

"Jose, we are not getting the police involved," Miguel told his son. He ignored Joe's protest and took the paper from the knife.

"But Dad, you have to call the police now. This isn't the first act of vandalism to happen on the farm. And this time it's much worse than someone stealing farm equipment. Somebody murdered our dog! Something really bad is going on."

"Who did this, Dad? And why?" Carmelita asked softly.

Miguel didn't answer; he was looking at the note. The words "THIS IS YOUR LAST WARNING, BERRY PICKER[i]. SELL NOW OR YOU WILL BE VERY SORRY" were written with letters cut out of a newspaper. Both of the children saw it, too.

Politically incorrect: **Berry Picker** ist ein abschätziger Begriff für die Einwohner lateinamerikanischer Herkunft in Texas, Kalifornien und Florida, da viele von ihnen als Gastarbeiter auf Erdbeerfeldern arbeiteten.

Carmelita let out a little cry, and Joe started to speak.
"Dad..."
"Save your breath, Jose. For the last time, no police! The cops are never on our side, and besides, the Alvarados take care of their own problems. Now, Carmelita, you go back to the house and get cleaned up. Jose, go to the shed and get an empty box for Hera. We need to bury her before the customers arrive."
"All you care about is your damned business!" Joe screamed.
Miguel ignored his son's angry curse. It wasn't true, but he would talk to Jose about it another time.
"And not a word to Rosa about this! I'll tell her myself."
"What the hell is going on here?" a woman suddenly shouted at them all. Rosa Alvarado had appeared suddenly at the edge of the field and was staring at the destroyed marigolds. Rosa was still wearing her pyjamas, and her long, curly, black hair was uncombed. She kept shouting as she walked towards them.
"I was trying to sleep, but I could hear you all the way back at the house. Miguel, why did you cut down the flowers – and Carmelita, what happened to you? And my God! Is that Hera?"

to kneel	knien
to save one's breath	sich die Mühe sparen
shed	Schuppen
to bury	beerdigen
to get going	*hier*: in Fahrt kommen
threatening	bedrohlich

Carmelita didn't even try to answer Rosa's questions. She pushed past her stepmother, and Joe was right behind her. The last thing either of them needed was one of Rosa's hysterical scenes.
Miguel tried to calm his wife down, but it wasn't easy. Rosa was almost 20 years younger than he was, and she had a fiery temperament. Once Rosa got going, it was hard to stop her. Miguel tried to hide the threatening note behind his back. But Rosa was too fast. She took it from him and read it out loud.

"Rosa, darling, I'm sure it's not that serious. It's most likely just teenagers playing a very sick joke. Please don't worry."

"Oh Miguel, really! I don't believe that for a second – and neither do you. We both know who is responsible for this! Sophie Martin-Woods has been after our land for years now. You keep saying you will never sell, but maybe you should change your mind. This is starting to get dangerous."

Miguel didn't correct Rosa's use of the words "our land". The farm was in his name only. He had refused to give half of it to Rosa when they had married. Miguel wasn't about to make the same mistake he'd made with Candace, his first wife. Buying out Candace after their divorce had taken every cent of his savings.

to be after sth.	hinter etw. her sein
to buy out	eine Abfindung zahlen
astonished	erstaunt
rudely	auf unhöfliche Weise
to interrupt sb.	jmd. unterbrechen

Exercise 3: Synonyms. Welche Begriffe gehören zusammen? Ordnen Sie zu!

1. ☐ surprise	a) get going
2. ☐ impolite	b) astonish
3. ☐ start	c) to be after
4. ☐ to try to get	d) rude

"We don't have any proof of that, Rosa," Miguel said and turned to look up at the office building towering over the field. "Now please go and get dressed. Look, a car is stopping at the stand. Our first customers are here."

"All right, Miguel. But this conversation isn't finished. Oh, before I forget, here's your phone. You left it by the bed - again."

Rosa handed her husband the smart phone she had given him for his birthday last month. It wasn't the newest version on the market, but Miguel still found it complicated enough.

Miguel watched his wife leave the field and started walking over to welcome the family of four waiting to pick their berries. Just then, his phone started ringing. Miguel looked at the display and was astonished to see who was calling.

"What do you want?" he asked rudely. "Don't you think you've caused enough trouble?"

The caller interrupted him. Miguel listened for a few moments to what they[i] had to say. His mouth opened wide in surprise.

"I have to go now," Miguel whispered his answer. "But you're right. We should talk in person. I'll be in my shed tonight around 8:00. Come by then, but be careful, and don't let anybody see you."

> Wenn das Subjekt eines Satzes, dessen Genus nicht bekannt ist, in einem weiteren Satz oder Nebensatz wiederaufgegriffen werden soll, so tritt an die Stelle der Personalpronomen **he/him** oder **she/her** das Pronomen **they** oder **them.** Da hier im Text „the caller" noch nicht näher bestimmt oder bekannt ist, steht „what **they** had to say" anstatt „what **he or she** had to say".

2 Netting Death

The business day on the farm went very well. By 5:00 p.m., all the ripe berries in the fields were gone. Only one little box of them was left on the stand. Miguel smiled as he counted the day's turnover. He estimated that after costs, the farm had made a profit of around $1000. He was very proud of his family. Carmelita had pulled herself together and kept the customers at the back end of the fields. Miguel and Jose had buried Hera and cleared away the dead marigolds. Then Rosa had come back, wearing a pretty summer dress. She also brought refreshments for the customers: homemade muffins, fresh lemonade and strawberry ice tea. This made the customers feel even more welcome and encouraged them to pick more berries. It was days like this that made Miguel even more certain that he was right to keep the farm. Then, the thought of how the day had started took the smile off his face. He hoped tonight's meeting would finally put an end to the vandalism. Lost in his thoughts, Miguel didn't see or hear Nathan Green walking towards him.

"Hey neighbor, how're things? I heard you had some problems again this morning. Sorry about Hera. She was a great dog."

Miguel wondered how Nathan had heard about what had happened. But then again, even back when they were boys, Nathan had always known the latest news and gossip.

"I'm okay, Nate. And you? Is business booming?"

Nathan worked as the in-house lawyer for the Laramie Group, one of the valley's largest investment and real estate firms.

"Can't complain, Miguel. But listen, the reason I came by was to ask you something. Have you heard from Candace lately?"

Miguel was surprised at the question. His ex-wife, Candace, was Nathan's younger sister. She had left Miguel for the city lights of San Francisco back when Carmelita was just a year old. Afterwards, Miguel and Nathan had managed to remain friends. The subject of Candace was taboo, though.

"Um, no, Nate. Why are you asking?"

"Just that she called me yesterday and sounded a little strange. I think she's sorry about leaving you – and the children, of course. Do the kids have much contact with her?"

Miguel just shook his head and quickly changed the subject.

"Sorry Nathan, but I have to get home. Rosa has dinner ready. Here, take the last of the day's berries with you".

"Thanks, Miguel. But I would like to talk with you again about Joe when you have time." Nathan saw the look on Miguel's face and corrected himself. "Sorry. *Jose*, I mean. Have you thought any more about letting him go to university next year? I'm sure I can help him get a scholarship."

"That's very kind of you, Nathan. But Jose's place is here on the farm. He knows that. This will all belong to him one day."

"Even if he doesn't want it? Miguel, your son's very bright, and I think he could go far…"

"That's enough, Nate! You're his uncle – but I'm his father. I know what's best for Jose. Now, good evening."

The Alvarado family ate dinner early. Rosa had made a taco salad, followed by fresh strawberries and ice cream for dessert.

to net	*hier*: etw. einbringen
turnover	Umsatz
proud	stolz
refreshments	Erfrischungsimbiss/-getränke
gossip	Klatsch, Gerüchte
ϟ business is booming	das Geschäft läuft gut
real estate	Immobilien
scholarship	Stipendium
bright	*hier*: intelligent

Exercise 4: Find the mistakes. Lesen Sie weiter und korrigieren Sie die sechs Fehler im folgenden Abschnitt!

Accept for Rosa, no one had much to talk at dinner.

"My meaning is that the threats are personnel. Confront Sophie!"

"Let's not discuss this now. Excuse me, I have work to make."

"Fine, Miguel. But if you're going to work long again, then I'll go and visit my sister. Carmelita and Joe, do you want to come, too?"

1. ______________ 4. ______________

2. ______________ 5. ______________

3. ______________ 6. ______________

Carmelita hesitated. Even though she didn't like Rosa that much, her sister Stella was nice. Carmelita said yes. Joe was dying to know what Rosa had meant by "confront Sophie," but he knew better than to ask his Dad now. Besides, he had other plans.
"Thanks Rosa, but I want to go to over to Alonzo's. Our study group is meeting there to work on our project, on the history of Silicon Valley. Dad, can I take the jeep, please?"

"Murderer!" Rosa was screaming again. Then she jumped up and ran at the woman standing in the kitchen doorway. It was obvious now who the other victim *wasn't*. Sophie Martin-Woods was alive, and Rosa was attacking her!
"You killed my husband. I know you did it!"
"You've completely gone over the edge, Rosa! Let me go!"
Rosa didn't listen. She started punching Sophie, and Sophie responded by slapping Rosa in the face.
Wilson knew he had to act fast. He grabbed Rosa, while the EMT pulled Sophie away. Then Wilson saw the red marks on Sophie's hands. They looked like burns! Shit, he thought. That could be proof that *she's* involved. Wilson had recognized Sophie. He knew she was a very, very rich woman, and famous, too. The last thing he needed was Sophie Martin-Woods as a suspect! Wilson knew he was going to need help and made a split-second decision.
"Listen to me, all of you! We're going to continue taking your statements down at headquarters."

Rosa, Nathan and Sophie all started protesting loudly, but Wilson ignored them. He'd just remembered that he had come in a fire truck. Wilson took out his phone to call for cars to come and transfer everyone to the DPS[i]. While he was waiting for an answer, he wondered if he should think about a career change. Putting out the fire had been the easy part of his night's work.
Wilson and three other police investigators finally finished questioning the Alvarados and Lisa at 7:00 am the next morning.

DPS steht für „Department for Public Safety". Fast jeder US-amerikanische Bundesstaat hat eine eigene solche Behörde. Sie ist unter anderem zuständig für die Verwaltung der Feuerwehr und der Polizei und anderen Einrichtungen der öffentlichen Sicherheit sowie für die Vergabe von Führerscheinen und Kraftfahrzeugkennzeichen.

Nathan had insisted on being present during the interviews with Rosa, Joe, and Carmelita. They had all gone home now. Sophie had refused to answer any questions until her own lawyer arrived. Wilson's supervisor was handling the VIP interview personally. Wilson was very glad about that. Now all the PSOs involved were waiting in a conference room for Assistant Chief Emanuel Barnes to finish and join them. Then they could compare notes and plan their next steps. After that, Wilson was hoping to go home for a shower and a couple of hours sleep.

Exercise 8: In other words. **Finden Sie in den beiden vorherigen Absätzen Wörter mit derselben Bedeutung!**

1. crazy ______________________
2. to act fast ______________________
3. option ______________________
4. proof ______________________

"Where's the coffee?" Barnes said, as he came into the room. Wilson poured his boss a cup, and Barnes got straight to the point. "First, I should tell you that we have to let Mrs. Martin-Woods go – for now." Barnes saw the skeptical looks on the team's faces and added, "That's a decision from the higher-ups."

"Her story," Barnes continued, "is that she called Mr. Alvarado last night, and he agreed to meet with her. She admits that she wanted to buy his farm and he had finally agreed to talk with her about it."

"But that means she was at the scene of the crime!" Wilson said.

"And how does she explain those burns?" asked Kim Song.

"According to her, she was almost at the shed when it exploded. She tried to open the door, but it was too hot. Then she panicked." Wilson found that hard to believe.

"But Manny, why didn't she report the fire, and why did she turn up later at the farmhouse?"

"She says she left because she saw Joe coming. And she came back after she saw her daughter's face on TV. She was worried."

Before anyone could comment on that, there was a quick knock on the door. It was a trainee PSO.

"Sorry to interrupt, sir. But Joe Alvarado's come back. He's very upset and says he has to talk with Officer Wilson immediately."

"Did he say what it's about?" Wilson asked.

"No. Only that he may know who the second victim is."

supervisor	Vorgesetzter
Assistant Chief	Stellvertretender Leiter (Polizei, Feuerwehr)
higher-up	hohes Tier
according to	laut, gemäß
trainee	Auszubildender

Exercise 9: People at work. **Vervollständigen Sie die Berufsbeschreibungen!**

1. A/An ________________ makes sure that other employees do their jobs.
2. A/An ________________ is in charge when the head police officer is away.
3. A/An ________________ is still learning how things work.
4. A/An ________________ is a VIP with a lot of influence.

4 A Network of Suspects

"Your Mom's missing?" Wilson asked Joe. The two of them were sitting in a small interview room. Joe was trying very hard not to cry. He felt like he was sleepwalking in some nightmare and couldn't wake up. He'd felt that way ever since the explosion.

"Yes, Officer Wilson. And I'm so afraid that, that she was in the shed with Dad last night! I tried to call her to tell her… tell her what happened to Dad."

"But you couldn't reach her?"

"No. She didn't answer on her cell[i], and she wasn't at home. Her new, um, partner said Mom didn't even come home last night."

> **Cell** ist die Abkürzung von **cell phone (cellular phone)**, der amerikanischen Bezeichnung für „Mobiltelefon". Im britischen Englisch ist hier vom **mobile phone** oder kurz **mobile** die Rede.

"And he wasn't worried about that?"

"*She* wasn't worried. My Mom's partner is a woman."

"Oh," was all Wilson could say at first. Then he decided that for now, Candace Green's sexual preferences weren't relevant. He also felt uncomfortable talking about that subject with her son.

"Joe, but still – what makes you think your Mom was in the shed with your Dad? Did they meet often?"

"No. They weren't on good terms at all. I, I think they had a kind of love/hate relationship. I'm sorry, Officer, but I don't know why Mom may have been with Dad. It's just a feeling. And it's strange that I can't find her." Wilson saw that Joe was about to lose control.

"Okay, Joe. You've already given us a DNA sample to help us identify your father. I'll give the order to compare your DNA with that of the second victim, too."

Wilson knew he might take some flak about that. The department's budget didn't have enough money to cover unnecessary and expensive DNA tests. And other than Joe's "feeling," there was no evidence that placed Candace Green in the shed. Still, Wilson's police instincts told him that it was a good lead. "It will take at least two or three days to get the DNA test results, Joe. Until then, we'll talk to your Mom's partner and her family, friends and employer. Maybe she's just gone out of town on a business trip."

to sleepwalk	schlafwandeln
to be on good terms with sb.	mit jmd. auf gutem Fuß stehen
to take flak	kritisiert werden
lead	*hier*: Hinweis
to comfort	trösten
exhausted	erschöpft

Wilson was trying to comfort Joe. But the words sounded empty, even to his own ears. He watched Joe walk slowly out of the office. The boy looked so sad and exhausted. That reminded Wilson of how tired he was. No chance of getting some rest now, though. There was too much work to do.

Exercise 10: Unscramble. Lesen Sie weiter und bilden Sie sinnvolle Wörter!

Wilson and his team worked **1.** ometrevi overtime the next several days. The hard work **2.** ffo piad paid off with lots of new

3. inmnotairf informations, but the investigators still had more questions than answers. Wilson was at his **4.** sked desk early Thursday morning preparing a **5.** snaipetronet presentation for the 9:00 a.m. strategy-planning **6.** sonsise session.

His report had three sections: 1. Facts, 2. Unknowns, and 3. Next steps. The "Facts" category included the DNA test results. The victims were now clearly identified: Miguel Alvarado and his ex-wife, Candace Green. The police also knew more about the means used to commit the crime. The bomb had been placed in a bag of inorganic fertilizer and ignited by remote control. Miguel's smart phone records showed that a call from an unidentified number came in at exactly the same time as the bomb went off. The police believed that the call had detonated the bomb. What they still didn't know was how the fertilizer had got into the shed or who had put the bomb in it. According to Joe, his father was strictly against using chemicals on the farm, and there was no record that Miguel had ordered such a fertilizer. With a sigh, Wilson realized the list of things under "Unknowns" was still way too long. We need to go back to the drawing board, Wilson thought. Under "Next steps" he added: "Brainstorm about possible motives, opportunities, and suspects."

means *pl*	Mittel, Methode
to go back to the drawing board	nochmal von vorne anfangen
opportunity	Gelegenheit, Möglichkeit

Exercise 11: Unscramble the sentences. **Bringen Sie die Wörter in die richtige Reihenfolge, um Wilsons Bericht zu vervollständigen!**

1. short what so we about give far learnt a have update

Give A short update about we have learnt so far.

2. such things not as discuss it know, did we who

Discuss such things we do not know such as who did it.

3. about session a hold factors brainstorming unknown team

Hold a team brainstorming fact session about unknown factors.

4. instructions steps questions and our for ask next give about

Ask for questions and give ~~about~~ instructions about ~~for~~ our next steps.

"Of course our main suspect is still Sophie Martin-Woods," Wilson told the team an hour later. "We know she was already making plans to buy the Alvarado farm so she could expand her business. Since Miguel Alvarado was refusing to sell, maybe she was behind all the threats – and the bombing, too."

"Yes, but we don't have real proof of that – yet," Song reminded them. "And if she did kill Alvarado, that doesn't automatically mean that she can buy the land. Do we even know those poor children's plans?"

"No. Their uncle, Nathan Green, is legally responsible for them until Joe turns 18 at the end of the summer. After that, he becomes his sister's guardian."

Wilson turned to the department's legal expert. "Anita, did you find out if Mr. Alvarado and Ms. Green left testaments?"

Anita Cole opened a file and put on her reading glasses.

"Yes. Joe and Carmelita inherit the farm from their father and half the money in his bank account. It's not much, though, and Rosa Alvarado gets the other half. Oh yes, she also has the right to live on the farm as long as the children don't sell it."

"Hmm. Did Mrs. Alvarado know about that?" Wilson asked.

"She says she did. And she claims that she didn't have a problem with it." Wilson raised an eyebrow. He had a hard time believing that any wife would be okay with practically being disinherited.

guardian	Vormund
to inherit	erben
to have a hard time	Schwierigkeiten haben
to make ends meet	über die Runden kommen
lump sum	einmaliger Betrag, Pauschale
shareholder	Teilhaber
to pop into one's head	jmd. plötzlich einfallen
murder-suicide	Mord mit anschließendem Selbstmord
to grasp at straws	nach jedem Strohhalm greifen

"I think we should have a closer look at Rosa Alvarado. Find out what the marriage was like, and check her background. So Anita, do you think that the children have to sell just to make ends meet?"
"No, Candace Green was very rich. She left her children a huge apartment in one of San Francisco's best neighborhoods. They will also receive a lump sum of cash and yearly incomes from her investments. She was a major shareholder in several very profitable companies. Financially speaking, Joe and Carmelita won't have any problems."
"True," Song said softly. "But emotionally, they're going to be in trouble. Especially if..." Song wasn't sure if she should tell the team what was on her mind. But during brainstorming sessions, you were supposed to say whatever popped into your head.
"Zach, I'm just wondering. What if Candace Green was behind the threats and the bombing? Her brother told us she sounded strange and depressed the last time he talked with her."
"That would mean it was a murder-suicide. But why?"
"I don't know – but I just can't think of any reason why she would secretly visit her ex in his shed. It just doesn't make sense. I guess I'm grasping at straws."

Exercise 12: Odd one out. Welches Wort ist das „schwarze Schaf"? Unterstreichen Sie!

1. inherit testament heirs lump sum
2. flak trouble suicide hard time
3. department shares headquarters office
4. lead means opportunity motive

At the farmhouse, Nathan was sitting with Joe, Carmelita, and Rosa. They all looked upset because they were discussing the funeral arrangements for Miguel and Candace. Rosa was trying unsuccessfully to stay calm.

"No! No! No! I told you, I won't let you bury my husband next to that woman!"

"'That woman,' as you call her, was our mother!" Joe cried out. "And it's not your decision, anyway! Tell her, Uncle Nate!"

Nathan felt horrible. He was in a very difficult position.

"Um, Rosa, I think the children's wishes should come first here. After all, they lost both their parents in this horrible fire. And," he added, "it's not like you and Miguel had the best of marriages."

"How can you say that, Nathan! I loved..." Rosa saw the look in Nathan's eyes and changed the subject.

"All right, do what you want. I know this isn't the best time, but I think I do have the right to know your plans for the farm."

Joe and Carmelita just stared at her. Rosa really was tactless.

Once again, Nathan tried to be the peacemaker.

"Rosa is right, children. She will have to move if you sell the farm. Even so, I think putting the farm on the market is the best option for the two of you. Both of you are far too young to own and operate a farm. And Joe, if you sell, then that means you could go to university."

"But Uncle Nate, I can go to university anyway. Remember? Mom left us enough money. We can hire someone to run the farm. And we could even afford to make some investments to make it more profitable."

funeral	Beerdigung
to put sth. on the market	etw. auf den Markt bringen
to hire sb.	jmd. einstellen, anheuern
to top sth.	*hier*: etw. überbieten

"And I will never agree to a sale," Carmelita said angrily. "Especially not to Sophie Martin-Woods. Dad hated her – and maybe she really did kill our parents – and Hera!"

"Oh Carmelita, don't be crazy!" Joe was also angry now. "You sound like Rosa. Lisa's Mom is a business woman, not a murderer! Besides, I saw her plans for the land, and I think Dad could have agreed. He just never had the chance."

"What do you mean, Joe?" Carmelita asked, a little more calmly. But Rosa didn't let Joe answer. "Nathan, why don't you tell the children your own ideas?"

"Um, yes. I can help you find another investor to buy the farm. I'm sure that I can use my business connections and get you a price that will top Sophie's offer."

Exercise 13: Find the money! Finden sie die zehn Wörter im Gitternetz, die mit Geld zu tun haben!

I	G	R	B	O	I	L	N	S	A
A	C	C	O	U	N	T	L	I	X
M	B	S	U	E	V	A	E	L	K
I	N	C	O	M	E	P	G	O	F
U	C	D	Q	U	S	E	A	L	I
M	A	R	K	E	T	W	C	C	N
O	S	B	Y	R	M	H	Y	S	A
L	H	U	A	W	E	I	M	R	N
T	A	Y	N	U	N	E	S	U	C
P	R	O	F	I	T	A	B	L	E
B	I	U	K	Y	C	R	S	M	E
L	D	T	U	R	N	O	V	E	R

"I'm sorry, Uncle Nate, but I don't want to sell to anyone! Not for any price! Joe, please, please, let's keep the farm. It's our legacy from Dad, and all we have left of him."

legacy	Vermächtnis

Carmelita started crying, and Joe took her in his arms.

"All right, Carmie, please don't cry. We don't have to decide now."

Nathan shook his head, a bit sadly.

"Actually, Joe, it's not your decision to make. It's mine. I'm your guardian, and it's my job to look after your best interests. I already have someone coming to look at the farm next week."

5 The Murderous Network

Joe couldn't sleep that night. His mind was too busy thinking about the awful scene with his Uncle Nate. They had had a terrible fight about selling the farm. Then Nathan had finally gone home, but not before he screamed at Joe and Carmelita: "You'll do what I tell you to do-end of the discussion."

Joe found the whole situation very bizarre. Nathan had always been a kind of mentor to him and had often taken Joe's side when he and his Dad hadn't seen eye to eye. And now this! It made him wonder and he lay awake for hours thinking about many other little things that had happened in the past. Sometimes, he had heard his Dad and Rosa fighting. A few times, he had also seen Rosa standing just a little, well, too close to Nathan. Finally, Joe got out of bed and went online. It didn't take him long to research the laws about guardianship in California. By the time the sun started to come up, Joe had a plan. He needed professional advice, but not from the police – not yet. He thought about taking the jeep, but he knew the sound of it starting would wake up Rosa and Carmelita. Quickly, he sent Lisa a text message. Then he got dressed and quietly sneaked out of the house.

to take sb.'s side	jds. Partei ergreifen
to see eye to eye	(völlig) einer Meinung sein
text message	SMS (Kurzmitteilung)
to sneak out	sich hinausschleichen

Exercise 14: Irregular Verbs. Lesen Sie weiter, übersetzen Sie die Verben und setzen Sie sie richtig ein!

machen | senden | trinken | schlafen | stehlen | sich streiten

Nathan also **1.** ____________ very much that night and was up early. The fact that he had **2.** ____________ with Joe and Carmelita was not what **3.** ____________ his sleep, though. The kids would come around – they had to. As always, Nathan **4.** ____________ himself a power shake for breakfast and **5.** ____________ it while checking his emails. His hands started shaking when he saw who had **6.** ____________ one of them.

He read it quickly, and the words on the screen scared him so badly that he dropped his glass. It shattered loudly on the terracotta floor. Nathan just left it there and ran upstairs to get dressed. Minutes later, he jumped into his company car and sped away. He had to act fast.

Officially, Officer Wilson had the day off. He'd planned to clean his apartment and then go to the gym. But the Alvarado/Green case was worrying him so much that he decided to work on it at home. Wilson started to turn on his laptop but changed his mind and got a notebook and pencil. It was old-fashioned, but sometimes the physical act of writing helped him to organize his thoughts. He wrote down several names and drew arrows between them to show how the people on his list were connected. Then he started playing a mental game of "what if?" This was something he'd learned to do at a professional development course last year. It was a way to think outside of the box. Basically, you just used your imagination and started speculating. Wilson decided to write down his "what ifs." After five minutes, he was surprised to see how many questions were on the page. The last one astonished him the most, though. Without really even thinking about it, he'd written down: "What if Nathan Green isn't rich?" I wonder where *that* came from, Wilson asked himself. He decided to follow up on the idea. In seconds, his browser gave him tons of hits for the key words "Nathan Green," "finances," and "investments." Wilson spent the next couple of hours reading and looking at photos taken of Green at various business and high society events. One picture was only two weeks old. Green was standing next to his sister, Candace. It was the look in her eyes that really got Wilson's brain working in a different direction. Spontaneously, he decided to call Candace Green's partner. Wanda Allan was a specialist in family law. If he was lucky, she'd be in her office now and not in court.

to come around	nachgeben, einlenken
to shatter	zersplittern
to speed away	davonbrausen
day off	freier Tag
professional development course	Weiterbildungskurs
to think outside of the box	über den Tellerrand sehen

Wanda Allan was in her office, but she wasn't alone. Joe and Lisa were sitting across from her. Joe had texted Lisa to ask if he could borrow her car to drive to San Francisco. She'd agreed, but insisted on coming with him. Joe had just finished explaining his concerns to Wanda.

"Well Joe, the law is quite clear on this. Even though your father named Nathan Green as your guardian in his will, the family court still has to sign off on it."

"And what if I don't want my uncle to be my guardian?" Joe asked.

"Any minor child over the age of 14 has the right to speak to the court about what they want. The judge will consider your wishes."

"So, my uncle can't make us sell the farm? At least not now?"

"No. In fact, the court has to agree that selling your inheritance is in your and Carmelita's best interests. Your uncle's a lawyer. He should know that."

will	Testament
to sign off on sth.	etw. genehmigen
inheritance	Erbschaft
relative	Verwandter
↯ to not want to go there	über etw. nicht sprechen/nachdenken wollen
to back out of sth.	aus etw. aussteigen
gambling debts	Spielschulden
persuasion	Beeinflussung, Überzeugung

Just then, the phone on Wanda's desk started ringing.

"Oh, Officer Wilson, what can I do for you?"

Wanda listened for a few moments; then, she asked Wilson to hold the line for a second.

"Joe, Officer Wilson is asking me about your uncle – and your mom. I really think the police should know about what you've told me. Will you tell him? Or should I do it for you?"

Joe looked at Lisa. He wasn't sure. Besides Carmelita, Nate was now his only close, living relative. But still, Nate was pressuring him to do something he didn't want to do and maybe he'd even…

Joe didn't want to go there.

"All right, Wanda. But you tell him, okay?"

"I'm telling you Nathan. Like I wrote in my email this morning, your time is up! Finish the job!" Abe Laramie was the CEO of the Laramie Group. His normally handsome face was red with anger.

"Abe, listen, just give me another week or so. Then the land will be yours," Nathan promised.

"That's what you told me last week. And last month. We can't wait anymore. Your brother-in-law is out of the way now, so what's the problem? Are you trying to back out of our deal?"

"No, Abe, of course not! It's just that Miguel's children need, um, a bit of persuasion first. I'm working on it."

"Oh, if that's all, then perhaps my partners and I can help."

"What do you mean by that?"

"I think you know, Nathan. I'd be sorry if something happened to your sister's kids. By the way, it's too bad about Candace. She was just in the wrong place at the wrong time."

Exercise 15: Make or do? Lesen Sie weiter und vervollständigen Sie die Ausdrücke mit der entsprechenden Form von *make* oder *do*!

Nathan had to be careful. He **1.** makes too many mistakes already. Two years ago, he **2.** had, did done something stupid and stolen from the company to pay his gambling debts. Abe had found out and offered **3.** to make a deal with Nathan.

At first, Nathan was only forced **4.** to do "little favors" for his boss. The Laramie Group **5.** did its main business by buying up top real estate. Then they resold it a few years later, **6.** making a huge profit.

When owners like Miguel didn't want to sell, Nathan had to convince them, even if that meant breaking the law. Acts of vandalism almost always worked, but not with Miguel. So Nathan had told his big sister about his dilemma at a reception a couple of weeks ago. He'd asked Candace to talk to Miguel. But Nathan had never even dreamed that doing so would lead to her death. In a way, it was all his fault. But he wasn't a murderer – Abe had other "helpers." Now all Nathan could do was try and keep them away from Candace's children. But he had to watch his words.

to convince sb.	jmd. überzeugen
to watch one's words	vorsichtig reden
nastily	auf gemeine Art und Weise
consider	betrachten

"Please Abe, just give me a few more days until after the funerals. The children are still in shock. They aren't thinking straight."
"All right. But your deadline, so to say, is next Wednesday. That's my last offer. After that, I want that land. Combined with your bit of property, it will be a real money-maker."
Abe laughed nastily when he saw the look on Nathan's face.

Exercise 16: Using new words. **Beantworten Sie die folgenden Fragen mit Vokabeln und Wendungen aus diesem Kapitel!**

1. Where can your boss send you to learn more about your job?
He can send me to a professional development course
2. If you look at a business problem in a different way, you are
to think outside of the box
_______________________________________ .
3. When you want to go on vacation, your supervisor must
sign of
_______________________________________ .
4. If you and a colleague don't agree, then you are not seeing
~~g to g~~ eye to eye
_______________________________________ .

"Oh, I forgot to tell you. You're going to sell me your place, too – at a discount. After that, I'll consider your debt paid in full."
Nathan thought carefully before he said his next words.
"Thank you, Abe. I'll get the job done – now."
Nathan left his boss's office with a little smile on his face. For the first time in months, he knew what he should do; what he *had* to do.
Nathan took out his phone and called Rosa's number. He'd been in love with her almost since the day Miguel had married her.

Nothing had ever happened between them, not really. But Nathan wanted to tell her what he had done and what he was going to do. Maybe she would wait for him. But Rosa's number was busy, so that would have to wait, too.

While he walked to his car, Nathan touched the tiny tape recorder in his pocket. It could never be used as evidence in court. In California, it was against the law to record a private conversation unless all parties agreed to it. But Nathan wasn't interested in using the recording as evidence. He just wanted it to help persuade the police that *he* hadn't set the bomb. On the way to his car, Nathan took out Officer Wilson's card. Then he looked one last time at the Laramie Group headquarters before he made the call. Wilson answered almost immediately.

parties *pl* — *hier*: die Beteiligten

"Officer Wilson, Nathan Green speaking. I need to talk with you."

"That's funny Mr. Green, I want to talk to you, too."

"Really? I think it's best if we do this in person, but somewhere private," Nathan told him. "I need to tell you a story about a network. A murderous network."

Manhattan Murder

Timothy Woods Palma

1 Wall Street

It is Thursday morning, and Detective Ted Quinlan walks quickly through the crowd. He is approaching his first destination of the day. In all directions are people of every shape, size and color. They are all scurrying to get where they need to go. Most of them wear suits. They appear out of taxi cabs and subway entrances. There are men selling things out of carts on the sidewalk: coffee, bagels, pretzels. It is rush hour, and this is Manhattan's financial district.

Exercise 1: Unscramble the words. Bringen Sie die Buchstaben in die richtige Reihenfolge!

1. inasdetonti destination
2. aarpep appear
3. merootp promot
4. ulhseedc schedule

"I'm not in Brooklyn anymore," Ted thinks to himself, looking up at the giant black tower of One Chase Manhattan Plaza. Today is only his fourth day on the job as an NYPD Detective. Before being promoted, he'd been on the force for nearly twenty years as a patrol officer in Flatbush, South Brooklyn. His wife, Dorona, and his two daughters are all very happy because the new position has a regular schedule and is safer and better paid. They might even be able to soon afford the summer house they've always dreamed of. However, this morning, here on Wall Street, Ted couldn't be further from a cozy mountain getaway.

On the thirty-second floor of One Chase Manhattan Plaza is the headquarters of a large multi-national corporation called Praxis Incorporated International, or PII for short. Detective Quinlan is downtown to see a man named Mekko Harjo, who works as an executive at PII. Harjo has recently become a suspect through material evidence in a homicide. Ted pushes through the revolving doors and enters the lobby. Inside, it is far less crowded than on the street and smells less like garbage. In fact, it smells like mint. Everything is clean. All the surfaces are shining. Yet, despite the relative calm, Ted feels uncomfortable. Wall Street, he has already realized, is a far more aggressive environment than any of the poor Brooklyn neighborhoods in which he has worked. He presses the button on the elevator, and there is a pleasant 'ding'. The doors open, and Detective Quinlan enters with a few others. He presses '32' and stands, a bit embarrassed. His suit is clearly of a lesser quality than those of the businessmen around him. The doors close, and they begin their ascent. As he has been doing incessantly for the past two days, Ted goes through the crime in his head:

to approach	erreichen, sich nähern
suit	Anzug
to appear	erscheinen
to promote sb.	jmd. befördern
cozy	gemütlich
headquarters	Hauptsitz
executive	leitender Angestellter
evidence	Beweis
revolving doors	Drehtür
ascent	Aufstieg, Fahrt nach oben

Early Tuesday morning, a woman's body was discovered by a boat passing under the Williamsburg Bridge. She hadn't landed in the water, but instead on a concrete island at the bridge's base. Dressed in a pink track suit, the body remained, at first, unidentified.

Exercise 2: Prepositions. Lesen Sie weiter und ergänzen Sie die fehlenden Präpositionen!

"This is often the case **1.** with runners," Ted had been told **2.** by his new partner, Detective Emily Peters. She's a veteran NYPD Detective, full **3.** of information, and happy **4.** to teach Ted her tricks **5.** of the trade. "They usually go running without their wallets or cell phones, so there is no form of I.D. We normally just need to wait **6.** till a missing person report comes in."

This is precisely what happened. An hour later, a man in Brooklyn named Zeke Virant reported his girlfriend missing. He had woken up alone in bed and found a note on the kitchen counter from the night before: "Gone for a run!" She was likely wearing a pink track suit, he explained. Her name was Marjorie Schillo.

When the elevator arrives at the thirty-second floor, Ted steps out. He is surprised by what he sees.

There is no one. It is just a large white and gray space, empty except for a fountain, a potted plant and three giant blue letters: PII. There is a set of frosted-glass doors, through which he can see the movement of silhouettes. They, too, are likely better dressed than he is. Ted pushes the doors open to find a receptionist behind a desk. She is young, with small features, glasses, and wears her brown hair pulled tightly back.

precisely	genau
likely	wahrscheinlich
receptionist	Rezeptionist
faintly	leicht, schwach
appointment	Termin
suspicious	misstrauisch

"Good morning, sir," she greets him. "How can I help you?"

Ted smiles back faintly and approaches the desk.

"I'm here to see Mr. Mekko Harjo," he tells her.

"Okay, sir, could I have your name?" she asks, still smiling. "Do you have an appointment with Mr. Harjo?"

"I'm Detective Ted Quinlan with the NYPD[i], and no, I don't have an appointment."

"Is Mr. Harjo expecting you?"

The detective shakes his head. "No."

Das **New York City Police Department** (NYPD) ist der Polizeidienst von New York. Es besteht aus zehn Abteilungen. Die Polizisten des NYPD (zwischen 35.000 und 40.000 Vollzugsbeamte) werden übrigens auch als **New York's Finest** bezeichnet.

Her eyes have grown wide and suspicious, and she begins to shift uncomfortably in her chair.

"Well, I'll let Mr. Harjo know that you're here. One moment, please."

Part of Ted is amused, but part of him feels guilty. The poor girl looks terrified. Perhaps she is new here. Or perhaps this is simply the first time a detective has ever come into the office of Praxis Incorporated International. Could it be? Ted hopes so. He would proudly be the first.

"Follow me," the receptionist tells Ted and leads him down a hallway to a door. She knocks and then opens it. Ted is taken aback by what he sees. The office is very bright, with floor-to-ceiling windows and a beautiful view of the harbor. Mekko Harjo rises from his desk to greet Detective Quinlan and shakes his hand.

"Good Morning, I'm Mekko Harjo."

"Detective Ted Quinlan. Pleasure."

"Please have a seat, Detective Quinlan," and Mekko gestures to the chair opposite his desk. But the movement causes him to wince, and he grabs his shoulder in pain. The receptionist closes the door behind her.

"What can I do for you today, Detective?"

"I'm here to ask you about your relationship with Marjorie Schillo."

"Marjorie Schillo?"

"Yes, Marjorie Schillo."

Mekko pauses, as if uncomfortable to go on, but continues.

"Marjorie Schillo, the physicist?"

Ted attempts to hide his excitement. Would it be this easy?

"That's right, the physicist. So you do know her?"

"Yes. We went to university together."

Ted looks over Mekko's shoulder. On the wall, a diploma hangs: Columbia School of Business.

"And have you seen one another often since then?"

"Not often. We've kept in touch, here and there. We were friends."

"When was the last time you saw Ms. Schillo?"

Mekko's face begins to show a sort of agitation.

"I'm not entirely sure, detective. But may I ask you why you're in my office right now asking me about a relationship with an old classmate?"

"So he wants to play hardball," Ted thinks to himself.
"Where were you Monday evening, Mr. Harjo?"
"I was in Boston, on business."
"You spent the night there?"
"Yes. At the Intercontinental Hotel. Why?"
"Well, Mr. Harjo, Marjorie Schillo was found dead two days ago, and it's looking increasingly like homicide."
Harjo's face drops, and for the moment his building aggression vanishes. It takes a moment for him to recompose himself and continue.
"That's very sad," he says, seeming genuine. "But, detective, what do I have to do with it?"
"Well, Mr. Harjo, we found a note in her pocket signed 'Mekko', telling her to meet him on Monday night, only hours before she was found dead."
Mekko swallows. For a moment, he is lost for words.
"I don't know what to tell you. I know nothing about it."
Ted stands up.
"Well, if you can think of anything to tell me, here's my card. And if you wouldn't mind, I'd like to call the Intercontinental in Boston, in order to verify your stay there."
Mekko rises as well, and they shake hands like they had when Ted entered. Only this time, Mekko isn't smiling.
"Y-Yes," he half stutters, "feel free to contact them."
Ted nods, eyes fixed on the suspect.
"Can I ask you one more question, Mr. Harjo? It seems as if you've hurt your shoulder. How did that happen?"

taken aback	verblüfft
wince	zusammenzucken
attempt	versuchen
agitation	Aufregung
ϟ to play hardball	mit harten Bandagen kämpfen
to vanish	verschwinden
to recompose oneself	sich wieder fangen
lost for words	sprachlos
verify	überprüfen

Exercise 3: Unscramble the sentences. **Bringen Sie die Wörter in die richtige Reihenfolge!**

1. building for aggression moment the vanishes his

   For the moment vanishes the aggression

2. what not to you do tell I know

   I do not know what to tell you

3. found pocket her in we note a

   We found a note in her pocket

4. across by quickest the river ferry is the way

   The quickest way across the river is by ferry

Mekko puts his hand to his injured shoulder and nods affirmatively.

"It's from a sailing accident last weekend in Montauk."

Quinlan nods. "Have a good day, Mr. Harjo."
"You too," Harjo responds and sits back down. He stares blankly out the window. As he closes the door behind him, Ted can see shimmers of the late morning sun on the river.
Walking away from One Manhattan Plaza, he is excited to be returning to his precinct in Williamsburg. He has a meeting over lunch with his partner Emily, who has just spoken to the victim's boyfriend Zeke Virant, and the quickest way across the river is by ferry.

affirmatively	zustimmend, bejahend
blankly	ausdruckslos
precinct	*hier*: Polizeirevier

2 The Bridge

The ferry pulls away from the dock at Wall Street and passes through the same sparkling harbor waters that Mekko Harjo can see from his office window. Perhaps Mekko's still looking down, Ted thinks to himself. He uses the free moment to call his secretary. He tells her about the Boston flight and hotel information and asks her to request verification.

Before long, the ferry is passing under the Willimsburg Bridge, right near the spot where the body of Marjorie Schillo had landed. Police tape still hangs on the concrete island. Ted looks up at the spot from where she must have jumped, or was thrown. But, if thrown, by who[i]? He thinks back to only two days ago, Tuesday morning, when he stood there with his new partner investigating his very first crime scene as a NYPD Detective. He remembers their conversation:

> Im amerikanischen Englisch wird oft **who** anstelle des Objektpronomens **whom** verwendet. Nach **by, for, with** steht normalerweise **whom,** aber **who** ist nicht immer unkorrekt.

"Do you think it's a suicide?" Ted had asked Emily, as they walked away from the crime scene and down the bridge towards their car. She shook her head.

"My gut instinct tells me no, but there's no evidence in either direction yet. Forensics will collect DNA samples from her clothes and from beneath her fingernails. But we also don't have any witnesses."

"You don't think that anyone will come forward?"

"Three-fourths of all witnesses step forth within the first few hours following a crime. So if no one has yet, there's only a small chance anyone will."
Ted was curious. "What about the other one-fourth?"
"They don't come forward at all, usually out of fear. They don't want to be the next victim, or they just don't want to get involved." Ted nodded.
"Especially in a city like New York," Emily continued. "People just want to be left alone."
They were interrupted by a voice coming out from beside a garbage can, where a homeless man sat holding a hamburger.
"Did you find him?" the man asked.
Ted responded. "Find who?"
"The guy in the purple trench coat," the man replied with a grin. "The one that was screaming at the woman last night."
Emily glanced quickly at Ted and then back to the man.
"What time last night?" she asked. "What did you see?"
His smile went away and he suddenly seemed angry. "Well if I tell you, what do I get out of it? Cops have never been nothing but trouble for me."
"We're not cops," Ted interjected. "We're detectives, and if you don't cooperate, we'll have to take you into the precinct. You're a witness to a possible homicide." He kneeled down towards the man. "So we hope you'll tell us what you saw."

spot	Ort, Stelle
gut instinct	Bauchgefühl
to come forward	*hier*: sich stellen
to capitulate	aufgeben, sich ergeben

The man capitulated. He didn't want any trouble.
"Well, it was pretty late, and I was sitting here, and I heard a woman's scream first, then a man's."
"What time was it?" Emily asked.

"Oh, I don't know," he said, motioning to his empty wrist. "I haven't exactly got a watch."
"*Approximately* what time," Ted amended sternly.
The man looked up to the sky, thinking. "Oh, I'd say, midnight."

Exercise 4: Past Tense. Lesen Sie weiter und setzen Sie die Verben ins Simple Past.

" **1.** Do ________________ you see the woman?" asked Emily.

The man **2.** shake ________________ his head. "No, by the time I **3.** get ________________ up to look, she was gone. I don't know where she **4.** go ________________; she sort of disappeared."

"But you **5.** see ________________ the man?" Ted asked.

"Only from behind. He **6.** wear ________________ a big purple trench coat and a big black hat and was walking down that way, pretty quickly."

"Towards Manhattan," Ted confirmed. The man **7.** nod ________________.

"Thank you very much for your help," **8.** say ________________ Ted with a smile.

They began to walk away, but Ted turned around.
"What's your name, sir?" he asked. The identity of a witness can make or break a case.
He smiled crazily. "The name's Richard Gluski." He took a big bite out of his hamburger. "But you can call me Ricky!"
"Richard Gluski," Ted repeated to himself, and they walked away, heading back to the precinct.
A few hours later, the coroner called. He informed them that he had found signs of a struggle: namely bruising on the victim's neck.
"They seem to be from strangling," he explained.

sternly	ernsthaft, streng
to make or break	entscheidend sein
coroner	Rechtsmediziner
to struggle	kämpfen
surveillance	Überwachung
property clerk	Immobilienkaufmann
to overlook	übersehen

"Were they masculine hands?" Ted asked, hoping for a push in the right direction.
"I'd say so," the coroner responded. "They aren't small."
At midnight, a strangling. A man, in a purple trench coat.
The bridge had no video surveillance, and the only witness was Ricky, the homeless man. Ted feared the case would go nowhere.
But the next day, Wednesday afternoon, Ted received a call from the property clerk that set the case in motion:
"Detective Quinlan, this is Richie Halter, from Properties."
"How can I help you, Richie?"
"I've got some good news for you, detective. It seems as if you overlooked a hidden pocket in the pink track suit of Marjorie Schillo. We were packaging it up for evidence when we found a note. I think it will help you out."
Ted became excited. "What did it say, Richie?"

"It said, 'My very dear Marjorie, meet me Monday night, same spot. Love, Mekko.'"

Bingo!

The detectives couldn't have asked for a more helpful name. There were only three Mekkos registered in New York City, and two of them were children.

So they had a suspect: Mekko Harjo.

Over lunch, Ted is feeling refreshed from the ferry ride across the river. He and Emily discuss all the information they've compiled thus far. Emily eats kale and miso soup as usual and tells Ted about the phone conversation she has just had with Zeke Virant, the boyfriend. He is not in New York, but in Pittsburgh.

"So he has already skipped town," remarks Ted. "Strange, isn't it?"

"He said he was with the Schillo family, preparing the funeral services. He told me he's practically part of the family. They'd been together nearly twenty years."

to compile	zusammentragen
to skip town	die Stadt wechseln
to claim	behaupten
rage	Wut
to elaborate	ausführen, ausarbeiten

Ted nods.

"But here's the thing," Emily continues. "When I mentioned the name Mekko, he acted very bizarrely."

"Bizarre, how?"

"Well, he began to stutter and seemed angry. And then he refused to speak any further, told me he was too busy and hung up."

"So you think he knows something?"

"Well, his tone was undoubtedly defensive."

Ted pauses. "He didn't say anything about knowing Harjo?"

"Knowing Harjo?" Emily is surprised by the question. "No, he didn't. You think Virant and Harjo know one another?"

"Well, Harjo told me that he went to Columbia with Marjorie, and that they were old friends."
"Really? But he didn't write the note?"
Ted shakes his head. "No, or at least he *claims* he didn't. But, if Mekko and Marjorie *were* having an affair, that would explain why the name Mekko got Virant all upset."
"True," Emily acknowledges.
"Do you think maybe he found out? Maybe he is the guy in the trench coat. A homicide of jealous rage?"
"We don't know enough yet," Emily says, "but we should keep our eyes open. Zeke is the last one to see Marjorie alive, and he's also the only one who seems to be withholding information. Unless you got something else out of Harjo?"

Exercise 5: Definitions. Verbinden Sie die Wörter mit ihren Definitionen!

1. ☐ come forward	a) engage in conflict
2. ☐ give in	b) make oneself known
3. ☐ struggle	c) refuse to give
4. ☐ withhold	d) surrender

Ted puts down the ham and cheese sandwich Dorona made him and elaborates for Emily about his meeting with Mekko at the PII office. He mentions Mekko's injured arm.
"An injured arm," Emily repeats. "That's very interesting. It would make sense that, if there was a struggle like the coroner said, the man might have been injured too."
"Did Zeke have any apparent injuries?"

Emily shakes her head. “Not that I noticed, no.”
Ted’s phone rings, and he picks it up. It is his secretary, and the news is disappointing. Emily can read it on his face.
“What’s wrong?” she asks him.
“The hotel in Boston supports Harjo’s alibi,” he tells her. “He checked in at 7 pm Monday evening and checked out Tuesday morning. United Airlines, too, verifies his presence on both flights.”

Exercise 6: True or false? Sind die folgenden Aussagen korrekt? Markieren Sie mit richtig ✓ oder falsch – !

1. Ted is a veteran detective.
2. Detectives Quinlan and Peters do not get along.
3. The witness on the bridge was not immediately helpful.
4. Zeke went home to Pittsburg to see his family.
5. Mekko lives uptown.
6. Dorona is Ted’s colleague.

“So he couldn’t have been in New York at the time of the murder.”
“Anything is possible,” Ted says, shrugging, “But as far as evidence is concerned, Harjo was out of town. We would need to find further evidence, somewhere else.”
The two sit there in silence, digesting their meals and considering their options.

trapped	gefangen
rarely	selten

"Next step?" Emily asks, a bit trapped in all the information.

"I suppose the only place to go is uptown."

Emily nods in agreement. "To Harjo's house."

So, Detectives Peters and Quinlan leave the precinct for their car. They're headed over the bridge and past the crime scene, then northbound up the FDR Drive[i], towards a place the two rarely go: the Upper East Side.

Mit **FDR-Drive** (oder auch **The Drive**) ist der ca. 15 km lange **Franklin D. Roosevelt East River Drive** gemeint, der an der East Side von Manhattan entlang des East River verläuft.

3 Uptown

It is mid-afternoon by the time Ted and Emily arrive on the Upper East Side. Heading cross-town towards Central Park, they pass many groups of children, all heading home from school.
"Does Harjo have any kids?" Emily asks, as they turn left onto Fifth Avenue.
"I didn't ask, but his file lists only one dependent: his wife."
Emily takes the file off the back seat, opens it, and reads aloud: "Meredith French, wife. Born: Dallas, Texas. 39 years old." She flips to the DMV file, which has a photo.
"She's very pretty," remarks Emily.
Ted pulls over in front of the address listed on Harjo's file.
"And very rich," Ted adds, looking up at 1117 Fifth Avenue.
Eleven-Seventeen Fifth Ave is across from one of the park's main entrances on East 90th. One can see through the summer trees to the famous gothic towers of the West Side.
They flash their badges at the doorman and ask for the way to Mekko Harjo's apartment, then take the elevator up to the twenty-first floor. The doors open up onto a foyer. They stand for a moment, examining the space. There are three doorways: one is to a hallway, one is closed and one is slightly ajar, emitting light. Ted peeks in, then gestures towards the door to Emily.
"It's a closet," he whispers.
Emily nods. She understands. Then the maid, a small Mexican lady wearing an apron and a baseball cap, enters.
"Ms. French wants you to wait for her in the drawing room," she tells them and points to the hallway. What they see through it is

breathtaking: a panoramic view of Manhattan, overlooking the park through the gigantic windows. Just across the street is an expansive lake, known as the Jackie Onassis Reservoir.

The maid walks to the far left side of the windows and begins to pull a curtain. The view suddenly disappears.

"Ms. French likes it dark."

Ted and Emily look at one another, as all the sunlight around them vanishes. They hear a raspy voice.

"Hello…"

They turn to find a very different woman from the one that they had expected. In fact, Meredith French is entirely the opposite. While her face still resembles the pretty one from the photo, it seems rather swollen, and she squints as if looking into the sun. She is dressed in a strange outfit. She wears a gray sweatshirt with a picture on it of a cat in a basket. Her pants are silver, and she wears an old pair of sneakers. Both the pants and the sweatshirt seem too tight, and Ted feels uncomfortable watching her move. She is holding a lit cigarette.

DMV (Department of Motor Vehicles)	Kraftfahrzeug-Zulassungsstelle
to examine	untersuchen
ajar	halb offen, angelehnt
breathtaking	atemberaubend
raspy	heiser, kratzig
to resemble	ähneln
swollen	geschwollen, aufgedunsen

"I'm Meredith French."

She lets the cigarette hang from her mouth as she offers her hand, which both Ted and Emily shake as they introduce themselves.

"How can I help you?" she asks. "I should say, I'm damned shocked. To be honest, I've never before had an unexpected visit from cops."

She takes a drag of her cigarette.

Meredith's voice is as shocking as her outfit. She speaks with a Texan drawl and a boyish roughness. One can almost hear the decades of smoking, like one can see it in her skin. Her speech is lazy and unrefined. She takes a drag of her cigarette.

Ted decides to do the talking. "We've been assigned to a case of possible homicide, and we'd like to speak to you about the whereabouts of your husband earlier this week."

"What? How has my Mekko gotten mixed up in a murder?"

"It's not yet clear whether the death was a murder or not, but we've had some leads, and we can clear your husband much quicker if you could tell us where he was this past Monday."

Meredith takes another drag of her cigarette and thinks.

roughness	Rauheit, Grobheit
unrefined	unfein, unkultiviert
to assign	zuweisen
whereabouts	Aufenthaltsort(e)
intercom	Wechselsprechanlage
pensively	nachdenklich

Exercise 7: Match up. Verbinden Sie die Wörter mit ihren Synonymen!

1. [b] conceal	a) inspect
2. [e] claim	b) hide verbergen
3. [d] resemble	c) upgrade
4. [a] examine	d) look like
5. [c] promote	e) assert bestätigen

"I'm sorry, I don't remember." Then she walks to an intercom and speaks into it.
"A beer please, Maria." She looks back at the detectives. "Would you two like anything to drink?"
They shake their heads no.
"Ms. French," Ted continues, "it would be a great help to us and to your husband if you could try and remember."
"Well, let me think." Meredith scratches her chin pensively. She takes another drag of her cigarette. "This past weekend, we were at our house out east, in Montauk."

Exercise 8: Articles. **Lesen Sie weiter und schreiben Sie *a, an, the* oder nichts in die Lücken!**

A door opens and Maria walks in, holding a can (Dose) of beer and 1. an empty glass on a platter. She offers them both, but Meredith only takes 2. the can. She snaps it open and takes 3. a big sip. Schluck

"Then we came home Sunday night." Meredith takes another drag of her cigarette. "And then we went to 4. / bed. In 5. the morning, I heard him leaving. I heard 6. the rolling wheels of a suitcase, so I imagined he was goin' somewhere on **7.** ⁄ business." She takes a sip of beer and another drag of her cigarette. "And then he came back Tuesday night," she explains.

Ted nods affirmatively.
"And where did he go on business?"
Meredith shrugs.
"I have no idea," she says and takes a sip.
The detectives look at one another. No idea?
Emily begins to speak.
"Do you mean to tell us, Ms. French, that you never asked your husband where he was going?"
"Miss..." Meredith begins, then pauses. "What's your name?"
"Detective Peters."
"Miss Peters, when your husband is practically absent from home *for a livin'*, you begin to lose interest in his whereabouts." A sip. A drag. "I don't really care if he was in Tuscon or Tampa Bay or Tasmania; it's all the same thing to me. I've lost track. So no, I cannot tell you where Mekko was, but I can tell you that he wasn't here, and as far as I know he wasn't in the city."
There is silence. Ted and Emily let the information sink in, as Meredith takes a sip of her beer and another drag on her cigarette.
Ted interrupts the silence.
"Do you happen to have a bathroom, Ms. French?"
Meredith nods and points.
"Yup, just head in back from where you came in – the first door on your left."
"Thanks," Ted offers, and heads exactly where he had hoped to go: the foyer. On the way, he peeks into the kitchen, to make sure Maria

won't be coming out. She is loading the dishwasher. Ted turns into the foyer and opens the first door to the left. Indeed, it's a bathroom, as Meredith said. However, he then tiptoes to the second door, which is slightly opened, and opens it a bit further: a large closet. It's rather disorganized and full of coats, shoes and hats. Ted's eyes scan the hanging garments: some winter coats… a rain slicker… several cardigans… a purple trench coat…
A purple trench coat! So Mekko *is* the murderer! But without a warrant, such evidence is useless. Ted slips into the small bathroom, flushes the toilet and closes the door loudly. When he arrives back in the living room Emily is alone, staring up at a painting above the mantelpiece: a grotesque and colorful portrait. Meredith has left the room.

to shrug	mit den Schultern zucken
practically	*hier*: so gut wie
to lose track	den Überblick verlieren
slightly	leicht
garments *pl*	Kleidung
mantelpiece	Kamineinfassung
to conceal	verdecken, kaschieren

"Find anything?" Emily whispers.
And Ted smiles, finding it difficult to conceal his excitement. "How many men in New York named Mekko own a purple trench coat?"
Emily smiles, still looking at the portrait. "Only one, I'd say."
Meredith reappears from a doorway and lights up another cigarette, takes a drag and begins coughing. Then the maid enters from the kitchen.
Through her coughing, Meredith asks, "Yes, Maria?"
"The landscaper from the house in Montauk is on the phone. He wants to know if you will be arriving this evening."
Meredith nods her head yes, still coughing, and turns to the detectives. "Is there anything more I can do for you?"

"If you don't mind me asking," began Ted, "where did you meet your husband, Ms. French?"

"In art school." She gestures towards the mantelpiece. "Believe it or not, Mekko was once a fine photographer."

And there, beside the portrait, hangs a black and white photo of a monkey in the middle of an empty room. Meredith flops down lazily on the couch. She grabs the remote and turns on the television.

"If there's nothing more you need," she says, "you can see yourselves out."

"Thank you, Ms. French."

And they leave.

In the car, Emily and Ted discuss their findings.

"So you saw the purple trench coat?"

"Yes, no doubt about it. And I can't imagine there being many of them."

to gesture towards sth.	auf etw. zeigen
to flop down	sich plumpsen lassen
remote (control)	Fernbedienung
to see oneself out	alleine hinausfinden
finding	Entdeckung
to confirm	bestätigen
to hire sb.	einstellen, anheuern

Exercise 9: Odd one out. Welches Wort ist das „schwarze Schaf"? Unterstreichen Sie!

1. shrug | gesture | ask | nod
2. foyer | drawing room | reservoir | closet
3. pretty | raspy | grotesque | swollen
4. low | confirmed | excitement | rich

"But both the hotel and the airline confirmed the alibi," Emily reiterates, "even if his wife cannot."

"Maybe he hired a look-alike," suggests Ted, "to go to Boston for him."

"Or maybe he hired a killer?" adds Emily.

"But why would the killer be wearing his purple jacket?"

"Why would you wear a purple jacket if you were going to murder someone in the first place?"

As they drove back downtown, the late summer sun was low above the skyline. In a few hours, it would set on another day of unanswered questions.

4 Murder She Wrote

It is Friday morning, and Ted is still at home having breakfast with Dorona and the children when his phone rings. He sees that it is Emily and picks up.

"Might I remind you," Ted begins playfully, "that it is not yet 8:30 in the morning, and I am technically off-duty."

However, it is no time for joking.

"Zeke is back in town."

"What?" Ted is caught off-guard. "How do you know?"

"He called me," Emily explains, "and he sounds terrible."

"I thought he was in Pittsburgh."

"He was, but he came home a couple of hours ago. He found some letters of Marjorie's."

"Letters?"

"Yes, letters," repeats Emily. "He says they prove who killed her."

Ted can feel the hair stand up on the back of his neck.

"Who?"

"I don't know. The connection was lost before he could tell me. Now, every time I call him back, there is no answer."

Ted thinks for a second. "Have you sent an officer to his place to check it out? The apartment is right by the precinct, isn't it?"

"To be honest, I don't want to lose his trust," Emily explains. "I think it's better if I go there myself."

technically	im Prinzip, eigentlich
to be caught off guard	überrascht/überrumpelt werden
uneasy	beunruhigt, unbehaglich
to be on edge	genervt sein
voicemail	Anrufbeantworter

This idea makes Ted uneasy.
"I don't know about that, Emily. You say he's on edge. Maybe it's better if I come along." But Detective Emily Peters is stubborn and a true professional:
"I appreciate your concern, Ted," she kindly responds, "but I've been doing this job for a decade. I have been in situations far more dangerous than this one. I'm going to head over to Zeke's place now, pick up the letters, and we can meet at the precinct in an hour."

Exercise 10: Subtle differences. Welcher Begriff passt besser? Ordnen Sie zu!

1. [a] to pick up the telephone — a) answer — b) respond
2. [b] to sound terrible — a) powerful — b) awful
3. [a] to prove something — a) reveal — b) tell
4. [a] to lose a phone's connection — a) reception — b) sound

At 9:30, Ted has been waiting at the precinct for fifteen minutes. He keeps looking at his watch. Emily is not the kind of person to be late without calling. He picks up his phone to check that everything is alright. The call goes straight to voicemail. He tries a moment later, but again, no answer. He will give her five more minutes, and then he will go over to Zeke's apartment.
Ten minutes later, Ted has left the precinct and is approaching Zeke's apartment. He sees Emily's car, an old, beat-up, red Ford Focus. He looks up into the window of the apartment. Suddenly, he sees a figure fly across the room, hears a crash and then a gunshot.

"Emily!" shouts Ted. He runs to the door, busts it open and races up the stairs.
When he arrives in the apartment, Emily is on top of Zeke, holding his wrists to the ground. There is a smashed lamp on the table, some broken pieces of pottery, and paper flying everywhere. There's a gun lying beside them.
"He tried to shoot himself. Grab the gun!" Emily shouts.

Exercise 11: Prepositions. Lesen Sie weiter und fügen Sie die richtigen Präpositionen ein!

over to from by with between

1. By late morning, forensics has already collected sample pages 2. from Marjorie's correspondence to verify the handwriting. The letters were, in fact, signed 'from Mekko', and documented the romantic relationship over the years 3. between him and Marjorie. The District Attorney's office has agreed 4. to issue an arrest warrant if the handwriting from the letters matches the one from the note in Marjorie's pocket. Emily and Ted are in the precinct, and she is going 5. over what she learned from her discussion 6. with Zeke.

"Why didn't you answer my calls?" Ted scolds her.
Emily explains herself. "I turned off my phone. Upon entering, I saw how sensitive the situation was."
"Was that before or after you saw a gun?"
"It's terrible!" laments Emily. "With those laws in Pennsylvania, Zeke was able to pick up a handgun as he drove home, without a license. He said he bought it to kill Mekko, but he couldn't find him."
"Because Mekko's in Montauk with Meredith, right?"
Emily nods. "Mekko's lucky day."

to race	rennen
wrist	Handgelenk
to scold sb.	jmd. schimpfen
license	Führerschein
to prove	beweisen

"Not if the letters prove that he's a murderer," Ted reminds her. "So what did Zeke find in them?"
"We'll need to read through them ourselves to verify, but as far as Zeke explained it to me, they prove that the affair had been going on for over a decade, since they all studied together."
"*All* studied *together*?" Ted is confused. "I thought Mekko and Marjorie were friends from Columbia?"
"That's what I thought, too. But in fact, all four of them studied together before that, at a small art school up the Hudson River. Mekko studied photography, Marjorie ceramics. Meredith was a painter, and Zeke was a musician. Zeke told me that he and Marjorie had been together since their freshman year[i], when they first met."
Emily paused. "Even more surprising, though, is that he told me Marjorie and Meredith were best friends all through school."

Ein **Freshman** (9th grader) ist ein Student im ersten Jahr. Im zweiten Jahr wird er zum **Sophomore** (10th grader), im dritten Jahr zum **Junior** (11th grader) und schließlich zum **Senior** (12th grader).

Ted cannot believe he had overlooked these details.

"And Zeke never had any idea of the affair?" asks Ted.

"Well, he claims not to have, but I don't really believe him."

"If he *had* suspected it, that would explain why he acted strangely when you mentioned Mekko's name to him yesterday."

"And," Emily adds, "why he rushed back to New York."

Ted is getting excited and growing impatient.

"How long will forensics take to match the handwriting?" he asks Emily.

"They said by tomorrow morning at the latest, but perhaps this evening. I told them it's necessary for a warrant, and they said they'd push it through as quickly as possible."

Ted walks over to the pile of letters on the desk and picks them up. There are dozens.

"So many letters," he remarks, flipping through them. They all begin the same way: "My very dear Marjorie…"

Two days earlier, when the initial note from Marjorie's pocket first surfaced, Ted had stared at it for a long time. Those two handwritten names were burned into his memory: "My very dear Marjorie" and "Love, Mekko." But now, looking at the tops of these letters, something seems strange. There is something wrong with the writing.

"Emily," Ted asks across the desk, "do we have a copy of the note? The one found in Marjorie's pocket?"

Emily nods. "Yes, of course." She opens the file and hands him a copy. Ted stares at the word "Marjorie" on the note and compares it to the "Marjorie" written in the letters.

Emily notices a change in Ted's face.

"What is it?" she asks.

"Come here," Ted tells her and places the papers on the desk. He points to the note from Marjorie's pocket.

"Do you see what the 'i' and the 'j' have in common?"

Emily looks at them. She notices a similarity.

"In the note from Marjorie's pocket, the i's and j's have little slashes on top of them..."

"Exactly! Little slashes," repeats Ted. "But lower-case i's and j's normally have dots above them, not slashes. It's as if whoever wrote this note let the pen drag each time he wrote an 'i' or a 'j.'"

Emily points again to the note, where 'meet me tonight' was written. Sure enough, in the word 'tonight,' the 'i' has a small slash atop it, where a dot would usually be.

Ted continues. "However, it's not the same in any of the letters that Mekko wrote to Marjorie over the years. You see," and Ted begins to point to examples in the correspondence. "Every time Mekko writes an 'i' or a 'j,' there is a dot on top of it. There is *not* a slash."

"Do you mean to suggest that someone else wrote the note in Marjorie's pocket?" asks Emily. "And that someone was *pretending* to be Mekko?"

"Well," Ted reminds her, "none of these letters are certified. We've no technical proof that they were actually written by Mekko until we hear from Forensics."

Emily walks over to the file and pulls out a document.

"Well this is his marriage certificate," she states, placing it on the desk in front of them. "It's one of the certified state documents that Forensics is using for the handwriting analysis."

Ted points to the left side of the certificate, where Mekko signed: *Mekko William Harjo*.

impatient	ungeduldig
warrant	Durchsuchungsbefehl
to surface	auftauchen
to compare	vergleichen
slash	Querstrich
to let sth. drag	etw. ziehen, schleifen lassen
to pretend	so tun als ob
to certify	bescheinigen, zertifizieren

"You see that? Above the two i's in William there are dots, not slashes."
"So someone forged Mekko's name and lured Marjorie to the bridge in order to kill her." She pauses. "But who?"
Ted thinks: What other man would want to kill Marjorie?
"Before this morning," continued Emily, "I would have thought Zeke, but now I don't think he would have hurt her."

Exercise 12. Unscramble the sentences. Bringen Sie die Wörter in die richtige Reihenfolge!

1. of | left | Ted | certificate | points | the | the | to | side

Ted points to the left side of the certificate.

2. walks | file | pulls | and | out | Emily | a | over | document | the | of

Emily walks over and pulls a document out of the file.

3. Marjorie | would | other | what | kill | man | to | want

What other man would want to kill Marjorie?

4. southern | can | Ted | drawl | suddenly | her | raspy | hear | and | deep

So Ted can suddenly hear her deep and raspy southern drawl.

As he considers the options in his mind, Ted's glance moves absentmindedly across the page to the right side of the marriage certificate. His eyes slowly scan the name signed there, and he is struck by what he sees. With slashes above the i's, in a handwriting unnervingly similar to that in the note from Marjorie's jacket, a name is spelled out. And Ted can suddenly hear her deep and raspy southern drawl: *Meredith Caitlin French*.

to forge	fälschen
to lure	locken
absentmindedly	geistesabwesend

5 The End

Montauk lies at the tip of Long Island: 100 miles east from New York City. To get there from Brooklyn, one must travel across the whole island. The trip, on a Friday evening in summer, can take hours and hours. But Emily and Ted, with their sirens sounding, will be there in no time. Neither detective lives in New York City proper. Rather Ted and Emily live in the suburbs. An NYPD detective's salary rarely affords him or her a home in their precinct.

Exercise 13: Correct the mistakes. Lesen Sie weiter und unterstreichen Sie die vier Fehler im folgenden Abschnitt!

Emily bought a house in New Jersey, over the Hudson River from Manhattan. Ted lives with Dorona and the daughters on Long Island. They therefore must drive about the expressway, right through Ted's town. As they continue passed it, Ted is reminded of how green and rural the island became. Soon, it feels as if their on the other side of the world. The setting sun behind them turns the passing fields golden pink and beautiful. It feels wonderful to be out off the city.

Just hours earlier, the case had come together perfectly. Almost immediately after Ted noticed the similarity in handwriting, they received a call from Forensics, who declared the analysis a so-called 'partial match'.

"The handwriting on the submitted note from the victim's pocket," the forensics officer explained, "only matched *one* of the submitted twelve pages."

"Which page?" Emily asked, confused.

The forensics officer elaborated. "It is a letter, dated 1993 and signed by someone named Meredith."

In the morning frenzy, they hadn't realized that the correspondence included letters from other people, not just those from Mekko.

"Also," added the officer at Forensics, "it seems like your DNA report has just arrived. I can have it sent to you with the handwriting analysis."

Sure enough, an hour later, the report arrived. Ted picked up the folder from the DNA department, and the result was another revelation:

"It seems like the DNA sample from under Marjorie's fingernails doesn't match the DNA of Harjo," Ted told Emily.

She was confused. "But how could they know that? We don't even have a sample of Mekko's DNA."

"No, and we won't need it," Ted responded, smiling at her. "The DNA from under Marjorie's fingernails is from a female."

Needless to say, the warrant for arrest was not very difficult to obtain.

salary	Gehalt
partial match	partielle Übereinstimmung
to submit	vorlegen, abgeben
frenzy	Rausch
revelation	Enthüllung
sample	Probe
to obtain	bekommen, erhalten

Exercise 14. Opposites. **Verbinden Sie die Wörter mit ihren Gegenteilen!**

1. ☐	to submit	a) to hide
2. ☐	to notice	b) to deprive
3. ☐	to hire	c) to withdraw
4. ☐	to afford	d) to lose
5. ☐	to obtain	e) to overlook
6. ☐	to reveal	f) to let go

The sun is setting over Montauk, and the maids have lit the candles in the dining room of Harjo's summer house. There is a large table and on opposite ends from one another sit Mekko and Meredith, in silence. All that is heard is the sound of silverware on ceramic plates and periodically the guzzle of Meredith's beer.

Mekko attempts conversation.

"Did you make it to the Guggenheim Museum[i] this week?" he asks.

Meredith takes a sip of her beer and a drag from her cigarette.

"No."

"The new modern photographers exhibition," continues Mekko, "is supposed to be incredible."

Das **Guggenheim Museum** befindet sich an der Upper East Side. Es wurde 1939 von Solomon R. Guggenheim gegründet. Vor allem Werke der Abstrakten Kunst finden sich dort, aber auch die Impressionisten und Post-Impressionisten, Expressionisten und Surrealisten sind vertreten.

Meredith says nothing. She takes a drag from her cigarette, and she burps.

Mekko tries again.

"I'll be in Dallas next week on business. Do you need me to pick anything up for you?"

Meredith takes the remote control from her lap and aims it like a gun at the large flat-screen above the electronic fireplace. It turns on, and a game show begins playing. She gets up from the table and crosses towards it, into the living room. She sits on the couch.

Mekko loses his temper.

"Damn it, Meredith. Talk to me!"

With that, the doorbell rings, and Mekko is distracted from his anger.

"Who could that be?" he asks himself, feeling a sudden dread. Meredith is looking up at the gameshow, unaffected by the sign of a visitor. They hear Maria's footsteps as she approaches the front door. The door is opened, there is the sound of Maria's pleas and a slight struggle. Then Maria enters the dining room, in from the foyer.

"Another beer, Maria," commands Meredith, her eyes still on the television.

But Maria looks terrified, and from behind her enters Detective Quinlan.

Mekko's anger returns.

"Detective, what, may I ask, are you doing here? Didn't the hotel and airline support my alibi?"

However, Ted isn't paying attention to Harjo. Instead, he approaches the entrance to the living room.

periodically	regelmäßig wiederkehrend
to burp	rülpsen, aufstoßen
to lose one's temper	die Beherrschung verlieren
plea	Bitte
to command	anordnen, befehlen

"Meredith French," he announces sternly and with pride, as Emily comes in from behind him, holding handcuffs. "You are under arrest for the murder of Marjorie Schillo."

Mekko proceeds towards the arrest, but Ted stops him.

"What the hell do you think you're doing? That's my wife!"

Meredith looks away from the television and stands up, sneering. "I didn't kill anybody!"

Emily begins to put the handcuffs on Meredith's wrists, pulling up her sleeves and so revealing five deep scratch marks on her forearm.

"And I bet you're going to claim those scratch marks aren't from Marjorie Schillo either?"

Mekko looks appalled.

"You little witch," growls Meredith, baring her teeth at Emily like an angry dog.

"Shut up," Emily demands, "and get your hands in these cuffs!"

Meredith allows her big, nearly man-sized hands to be locked into the handcuffs

Ted adds his two cents: "Get that scum out of here!" he calls out, and Meredith is taken out to the police car.

They exit. Their job is finished.

There are certain things that make up for the danger involved in being a detective. These things make up for the long hours and the relatively bad pay. Mekko Harjo, a corporate executive, does very little to help the world or support the safety of society, and yet he earns ten times the salary that Detective Quinlan does.

to sneer	höhnisch lächeln
to reveal	erkennen lassen, zeigen
appalled	erschrocken, entsetzt
to bare one's teeth at sb	jmd. die Zähne zeigen
to add one's two cents	seinen Senf dazugeben
to make up for	wieder gut machen
lawn	Rasen
wealth	Reichtum

Exercise 15: Idiomatic expressions. Übersetzen Sie die folgenden Wendungen ins Englische!

1. genervt sein ____________________
2. die Beherrschung verlieren ____________________
3. seinen Senf dazugeben ____________________
4. jemandem die Zähne zeigen ____________________

However, as Mekko cries on the front lawn of his giant summer home, Ted is not jealous of his wealth or his status. For today, Ted has experienced the euphoria of solving a murder case and of seeing the criminal put behind bars.

Luckily for the detectives, Meredith was very open and honest about the homicide once she realized she had been caught. She admitted to it immediately, a bit like a lunatic.

"Yeah, so I killed her!" she yells, as her head is being shoved into the back of the police car. "And I'd do it again!"

Her voice is even raspier and less forgivable than normal. The detectives watch the police car drive away and then cross the street to the beach. They walk in the sand towards the shore. Their job for the day is done, and they can breathe a bit easier.

"I can't believe we didn't see it sooner," Ted remarks. "I mean, it should have been so obvious."

"But, of course, it wasn't." Emily reminds him, "We had the witness stating it was a man. We had a coroner who said the hands were masculine. We had a note signed by Mekko. Why would we have ever suspected a woman?"

Ted shook his head. "Yes, but Meredith was not a normal woman. I should have taken that into account."

Emily smiled. "You solved your first case," she reminded him. "You're a great detective, and you will only get better."

"Thank you," he offers, and looks out over the water.

to take sth. into account	etw. berücksichtigen
to solve	lösen

"It's been a busy first week for you, hasn't it?" Emily comments. She is proud of her new partner. He nods and, with a smile, thinks: "I look forward to my second."

Exercise 16: Past progressive. Setzen Sie die unterstrichenen Satzteile in die Verlaufsform der Vergangenheit.

1. As Ted and Emily <u>drive</u>, their sirens <u>sound</u>.

____

2. The sun <u>sets</u>, and the maids <u>light</u> the candles.

____

3. Mekko <u>feels</u> a sudden dread.

____

4. I <u>look</u> forward to my second.

____

Murder Made Easy

Gina Billy

1 Easy Come, Easy Go

Lauren LeBlanc knew that Central City wasn't one of New Orleans' nicer neighborhoods. But still, the sight of all the empty houses and mountains of garbage everywhere surprised her. There were very few people around. And those she did see were walking quickly and trying not to make eye contact. There were no signs here of the carnival celebrations taking place in other parts of the city. But everywhere Lauren looked, she could see evidence of damage done back in 2005 by Hurricane Katrina. Even though the late Thursday afternoon in February was quite mild, Lauren suddenly felt cold. She turned to the man walking next to her on Clio Street. Unlike her, Leroy Harris was a "Big Easy"[i] native. But he also didn't seem to feel comfortable being here. "Leroy, are you sure this is the right place?"

> **The Big Easy** ist einer von vielen Spitznamen der Stadt New Orleans. Weitere Namen der Stadt sind **NOLA** (New Orleans, Lousiana), **The Crescent City** (weil die Stadt die Form einer Mondsichel hat), **The City That Care Forgot** (wegen der Sorglosigkeit der Menschen in New Orleans) und **Mogadishu on the Mississippi** (Vergleich mit der somalischen Hauptstadt wegen der hohen Kriminalität).

"This is it, Lauren. Look, you can see the Mercedes-Benz Superdome from here, just like our informant told us."

Leroy Harris pointed to the top of the famous sports arena. It stood out clearly in the distance behind the loud Ponchartrain Expressway.

“See that house between the two vacant lots? That must be where we’re meeting him.”

The old wooden house Leroy was pointing at must have been beautiful once. But now all its windows were broken, and the paint was all but gone. The house looked like it was about to fall down, and Lauren couldn’t imagine anyone living there. “All right, Leroy, if you say so. You’re the boss.”

“Lauren, for the last time, I’m just a photographer. You’re the reporter here, so that means you’re in charge.”

“Yeah, Leroy – but you’re the one who had the idea for the story we’re researching. And, the informant contacted you, not me. Besides, I’m still a rookie. You’re the real pro here, and, poor guy, you got the assignment of showing me the ropes.”

evidence	Beweise
vacant lot	unbebautes Grundstück
rookie	Berufseinsteiger
assignment	Aufgabe
to show sb. the ropes	jmd. einarbeiten
whistleblower	Informant

“Well, there are worse jobs,” Leroy said with a smile.

Lauren wasn’t only new to NOLA, she also didn’t have much experience in the world of television news. At WNEO–TV, everybody said that Lauren had got the job because of her blonde good looks. At first, Leroy hadn’t been happy about having to babysit the new girl from Mississippi. But Lauren had quickly shown that she was a lot more than a very pretty face. That’s why he’d decided to share the secret information with her.

“Okay, Leroy. Turn on the hidden camera then, and let’s go.”

“No Lauren! Jul…I mean, the informant doesn’t want to be filmed.”

“Leroy! Do you *know* our whistleblower?”

“No, of course not. I just…” Leroy stopped speaking. The front door of the house was starting to open. A very tall, African-Amer-

ican man put his head out of the door and looked carefully to the right and left. When he saw Lauren and Leroy, he stepped quickly back inside. But he left the door open, and Lauren could just barely see him standing there in the entryway.
She decided to ask Leroy about his interesting slip up later.
"Look, Leroy, we won't use the pictures. I promise. But I want to play it safe here, so please – start recording."

Exercise 1: Three-way matching. Welche der folgenden Wörter passen am besten zusammen? Ordnen Sie zu!

1. ☐☐ trainer	a) in charge	e) learns on the job
2. ☐☐ rookie	b) informant	f) head
3. ☐☐ boss	c) new	g) reveals secrets
4. ☐☐ whistleblower	d) experience	h) shows ropes

Leroy put his hand inside the small bag where the camera was hidden. Lauren was right. This story was a very hot one, and they might need the footage to prove it. He'd explain it to Julian later. The two journalists started to cross the old-fashioned stone street. Lauren didn't see the pieces of old, abandoned streetcar tracks until it was too late. One of her high heels got caught on the rails and she tripped. Leroy tried to catch her, but missed, and Lauren fell hard on her knees. The man in the doorway started coming out again just as Leroy was bending down to help Lauren up. Suddenly, they heard loud staccato pops that sounded like fireworks. But they weren't and the few people on the street knew it and began running for safety. The man in the doorway managed to shout:

"Leroy! Ya'll get the hell out of here!"
Then there was more gunfire and his shouting became a scream of pain – and then, silence.
Lauren tried to get up and run to him, but Leroy stopped her.
"Are you crazy? We have to get out of here quickly, Lauren. The police will arrive soon, and we don't need them to find us here."
"But Leroy, we have to help our informant. Call an ambulance and the newsroom. We can do a live report from here!"
Leroy put a hand over her mouth and pulled her to him.
"Lauren, look at him! It's too late to help."
Leroy turned Lauren's head so that she could see the man lying face down in a pool of blood on the front steps. He wasn't moving.
"The first rule of journalism is: Live to tell the story! The shooter may still be around somewhere, and remember why we're here. In NOLA, the police can be more dangerous than the criminals. Now keep your mouth shut and follow me!"

slip up	Versehen
to play it safe	auf Nummer sicher gehen
footage	Filmmaterial
abandoned	*hier*: ausrangiert, verlassen
ϟ ya'll (you all)	ihr, euch (Südstaaten-Dialekt)
homicide	Mord
victim	Opfer
case load	Anzahl der Fälle

Half an hour later, Detective Calliope Carollo stared down at the dead man and shook her head sadly. Another homicide in Central City. And this one had the same profile as most of the other victims in her heavy case load: Young. Black. Male. He could have been her own son. And he was what? The 40th murder victim in NOLA this year. Shit, it was only the middle of February! It looked like the "Big Easy" was living up to one of its other nicknames, "Mogadishu on the Mississippi." NOLA had one of the highest murder and other violent crime rates in the United States.

"Hey, Cal! See what Leon's found!"

Calliope looked at the two plastic bags filled with white powder that her partner was holding. Detective Clovis Dufrene had a big smile on his fat, light-brown face. Calliope hated being called "Cal", and Clovis knew it. But she decided to let it go – for now.

Exercise 2: Asking questions. Lesen Sie weiter und ergänzen sie die Fragen mit der richtigen Form der fehlenden Hilfsverben!

be (2 x) have do (2 x)

"So, what **1.** ______ you think, Clovis?

2. ______ it another drug deal gone bad?"

"Well, I'll bet my next pay check that this stuff is cocaine."

"Where **3.** ______ Hart find it?"

"Hidden upstairs in a broken toilet. Not very original."

"**4.** ______ there any sign of gang involvement?"

"We haven't found any, yet. But where there are drugs..."

"Yeah, I know. **5.** ______ we got an ID?"

"We found a driver's license. The photo looks like him – before he got a bullet through the head. Julian Fortune, age 26."

Clovis pronounced the surname the NOLA way: For-tu-nay.

Just then another police officer came slowly out of the house. Officer Leon Hart looked tired, as always. Calliope knew that like many NOLA police officers, he moonlighted as a security guard.

"Detectives, have a look at this. Guess our guy was a dealer, not a user."

Hart had an evidence bag filled with money.

"How much is it?" Calliope asked.

"I, um, haven't counted it yet. The new SOPs say I have to do that in front of a witness."

"Yes, well Leon, the rule also says that you are supposed to leave monetary evidence where you find it. You have to bag it in front of a witness, too."

"Oh sorry, Calliope," Clovis apologized. "I forgot to mention that. I was there when Leon put the cash in the bag. I'll count it now."

Calliope thought that was a bit strange. They could have counted the money before they bagged it. But to be honest, she didn't really want to know, and sometimes, it was better not to rock the boat. When Clovis finished counting, he smiled again. Then he held the money over the victim's head.

"Well, Mr. Julian Fortune, I guess your own little fortune was 'easy come, easy go'," he said with a laugh. But a voice calling from across the street took the smile off his face.

"Detective! Is that how the NOLA police deals with crime victims?"

to live up to sth.	etw. gerecht werden
nickname	Spitzname
to let sth. go	etw. auf sich beruhen lassen
pay check	Gehaltscheck
to moonlight	nebenbei schwarzarbeiten
SOP (Standard Operating Procedures)	Standardarbeitsanweisungen
witness	Zeuge
to rock the boat	für Ärger sorgen
easy come, easy go	wie gewonnen, so zerronnen

It was Lauren, and Leroy was right behind her. He had the camera on his shoulder now. The two of them had gone around the corner and waited half an hour before returning to the crime scene. During that time, Leroy had explained his plan to Lauren.

"How did you two get past the police barricade?" Clovis asked angrily.

"Oh, just a trick of the trade," Lauren told him sweetly. "We were already in the neighborhood working on another story."

Calliope hated dealing with reporters, but she was the Senior Detective. And her partner needed saving from his own stupidity.

"Excuse me, you're new with WNEO-TV, aren't you?"

"Yes, Detective. I'm Lauren LeBlanc, I've just transferred from our sister station in Jacksonville, Mississippi."

"Well, Ms. LeBlanc, reporters aren't allowed at NOLA crime scenes. You have to wait for interviews with the other media."

"But Detective, can't you comment on your colleague's behavior?"

Calliope thought quickly. It was against the rules, but it seemed like she had no choice but to respond.

"Detective Dufrene's action was disrespectful, and I'm certain he will get an official reprimand and of course, apologize. Clovis?"

"Yes, I'm very sorry. But we believe the victim was a coke dealer. And I guess it's hard for me to feel sorry for someone like him."

"I want to ask you one thing," Calliope said. "Don't use your footage until after we inform the victim's family. If you agree, I'll give you an exclusive interview in a couple of days."

Lauren and Leroy looked at each other for a moment.

"All right Detective," Lauren said. "We have a deal."

trick of the trade	Handwerkskunststück
senior	*hier*: leitend, ranghoch
to transfer	*hier*: umziehen, versetzen
reprimand	Verwarnung

Exercise 3: Definitions. **Beschreiben Sie die Definitionen mit einer Vokabel aus dem Text!**

1. to have another job besides your main job:

   ____

2. to move from one job or place to another:

   ____

3. the official rules, ways of doing something:

   ____

4. verbal or written complaint for misbehavior:

   ____

2 Easier Said than Done

Lauren and Leroy's short report about the latest Central City murder wasn't the first story on the evening news. There had been another, more sensational killing that day. A tourist from Florida had been robbed and stabbed to death in the French Quarter. This was not the kind of news the city needed – especially so close to Mardi Gras[i]. Lauren watched the report from WNEO's award-winning crime reporter, Vincent Mercier, with Leroy in the employee break room. It was followed by a live interview with the city's mayor. He was promising to increase police patrols to keep the public safe during Carnival.

> **Mardi Gras** ist die französische Bezeichnung für „Faschingsdienstag". Wörtlich übersetzt heißt es „fetter Dienstag". Die Tradition wurde von französischen Katholiken in die damalige französische Kolonie Louisiana gebracht. Da ein schöner Brauch sich lange hält, wird noch heute der Dienstag vorm Aschermittwoch (Ash Wednesday) gefeiert und damit die Fastenzeit eingeläutet.

"Leroy, do you think Mayor Guidry suspects – or even knows – what's going on in the police department?" Lauren asked.

"I don't know, Lauren. But Rene Guidry is a really big fish, and finding the answer is easier said than done."

Before the two of them could discuss it further, one of the station's interns opened the door and almost ran inside.

"Hey, ya'll. Ava wants to see you in her office, on the double."

Ava Clark was the producer directly responsible for all stories that dealt with crime. She was also the only other person on the news team that knew about what Lauren and Leroy were working on. But when Leroy and Lauren had returned from Central City, Ava had been too busy with the tourist murder story to talk with them. So they had prepared their report without her input. Lauren had kept to the facts that Detective Carollo gave during the official press conference. Leroy hadn't used any of the footage from the hidden camera or the crime scene. They were keeping that for their other, bigger story about large-scale corruption in the police department. But now that the informant was dead, their story might be dead, too.

Mardi Gras (Fat Tuesday)	Faschingsdienstag
to suspect	verdächtigen
big fish	hohes Tier
intern	Praktikant
on the double	sofort

Exercise 4: Choose the right word. Lesen Sie weiter und unterstreichen Sie die richtig Variante!

When Lauren and Leroy got to Ava's **1.** bureau / office , the door was open. The producer had short, curly red **2.** hairs / hair that was almost as untidy as the **3.** writing table / desk she was sitting behind. Four TVs were turned on at full **4.** volume / sound . Ava was **5.** looking / watching different news reports at the same time.

"Thank goodness you're okay!" she said when she saw them. "I should reprimand you about being late for the interview with your informant. But in this case, it's lucky you were. The two of you could have been killed! Now tell me what happened."

Lauren thought Leroy should do the talking. He knew Ava better, and after all, it was really his story. When he kept quiet though, she stepped on his foot with one of her heels. It worked.

"Well, Ava. We weren't late. Lauren and I saw the whole thing, and I have it on video!"

"What? You have footage of our informant being murdered? Why didn't you tell me this before? Let me see it!"

Leroy gave Ava the camera's memory card. She motioned for them to pull up chairs as she put the card into her computer. The pictures were a bit shaky, especially when the shooting began and people started running. But the informant could clearly be seen and heard. Lauren closed her eyes when the bullets hit him.

"This is dynamite, Leroy," Ava praised him.

"Excellent work. But now tell me the truth, did you know him?"

It was time for Leroy to come clean – but it was hard. He knew that Ava and Lauren would both be angry. He had lied to them.

"Yes. I knew Julian Fortune, but not that well. We used to live in the same area and played football together at high school. I hadn't seen him in years, though."

"Oh Leroy, I'm so sorry!" Lauren took his hand. "How horrible for you to have to watch your friend die."

"Me, too, Leroy, but you're a hardened professional. What I want to know is, why didn't you tell me – us – this before?"

"Julian made me promise to keep his identity secret. He was also a bit paranoid. He said if anyone found out that we knew each other, they wouldn't believe me. And that I'd be in danger, too."

"Well, he was right about that," Lauren said slowly. "Do you think Julian was killed to keep him from talking to us?"

"Maybe, maybe not," Ava answered. "The real question is, what are we going to do now? No Julian, no story. He was the only one we know of who supposedly had proof about the deals the police are making with the area gangs."

That was at the heart of the journalists' investigations. According to Julian, the police were taking kickbacks from gang leaders involved in drug trafficking. In exchange for the large amounts of money, the police turned a blind eye to the gangs' criminal activities. Julian had told Leroy he had hard evidence that the corruption went all the way to the top brass.

"Did Julian give you any idea about what kind of proof he had? Ava asked. "Or how he got it?"

"I don't know what he had, Ava. That's what he was going to tell us today. But I know for sure what he didn't have. Julian hated drugs. He would never have taken or dealt in cocaine. I don't believe the police story of a drug deal gone wrong for a minute! But proving that is easier said than done."

"So what are you thinking, Leroy?" Ava pushed her chair back and stood up. "Could the police have put the coke there? Or was it somebody else? Or maybe you just didn't know your friend as well as you think you do."

Leroy stood up, too. He tried not to show how angry he was.

"Ava, can we do this tomorrow? It's been one shitty day. I really want to call it a night and go have a beer – or three. How about you, Lauren?"

to praise	loben
to come clean	auspacken
hardened professional	harter Brocken
supposedly	angeblich
kickbacks *pl*	Bestechungsgelder, Schmiergeld
to turn a blind eye	ein Auge zudrücken
top brass	die da oben
to call it a night	Feierabend machen

Lauren felt a bit conflicted. She suddenly realized how exhausted she was. And Leroy wasn't just a colleague; he was also an extremely good-looking man. It would be nice to get to know him better over a couple of drinks. But she was new here and in some ways, Ava was her boss. Lauren didn't want to get on her bad side. Fortunately, Ava made the decision for her.

"Good idea, Leroy. You two go take it easy. We'll talk again in the morning and decide what to do with the footage then."

"What do you mean by 'do with it'?" Leroy asked. Suddenly, he was worried that Ava might use it in a story. Then he and Lauren would be in big trouble for lying to the police.

"Well, technically speaking, we should give it to the cops. It's evidence in Julian's murder. We're going to need advice from the legal department on that one. For now, I'll lock it in my safe."

Exercise 5: Opposites. Finden Sie im vorhergehenden Abschnitt das Gegenteil von folgenden Ausdrücken!

1. to keep on working __________
2. to not tell the truth __________
3. to criticize __________
4. to pay attention to __________

Leroy took Lauren to the city's oldest, still-operating jazz club. Even though it was in the middle of the French Quarter, Fritzel's Jazz Pub was cozy and not touristy. The traditional Dixie Land Band was very loud, so Lauren and Leroy didn't even try to talk above the music. Instead they sat at a table in the back behind the dance floor and drank German tap beer that Fritzel's had on offer. Lauren also enjoyed looking at the Carnival decorations and costumes that the staff and many customers were wearing. By the time the band was ready for a break, both of them felt more relaxed. The recorded music playing now was quieter.

"Lauren, let's not talk shop. Tell me more about yourself and what you think of the Big Easy."

"Oh, I think the city is fascinating. The people are so full of life, and most of them are really kind and helpful. But shootings like the one today scare me."

to get on sb.'s bad side	sich bei jmd. unbeliebt machen
technically speaking	genau genommen
tap	vom Fass
staff	Belegschaft, Mitarbeiter
to talk shop	fachsimpeln
so-called	angeblich, so genannt
to attract	anziehen, reizen
policy	Grundsätze, Strategie

"Well, you do have to be careful here in the so-called 'City that Care Forgot.'"

"Is that another nickname for New Orleans?" Lauren asked. "It has so many! But that one isn't really true anymore. The city has so many problems – especially since Hurricane Katrina [i]."

Lauren suddenly stopped speaking and took Leroy's hand. Wow, he thought, is she flirting with me? Part of him hoped so because something about Lauren really attracted him. She bent her head towards him. Maybe he should rethink his policy about not getting

Hurricane Katrina war ein Wirbelsturm von verheerendem Ausmaß, der 2005 in den Bundesstaaten Florida, Louisiana, Mississippi, Alabama und Georgia erhebliche Schäden anrichtete und insgesamt ca. 1800 Todesopfer forderte. **New Orleans** wurde dabei besonders hart getroffen.

involved with women at work. But the words Lauren whispered in his ear had nothing to with love.

"Leroy, don't turn around! Detective Dufrene and Officer Hart just came in with some other men. They're going up to the bar."

Leroy was disappointed at first because work was getting in the way of pleasure *again*. Then his professional instincts took over.

"That's very strange," he whispered back. "Fritzel's is not a usual hang-out for cops. Admission is free, but the drinks are too expensive." He risked taking a quick look towards the bar.

"The guys with them are cops, too. Except for the really short one. He looks familiar. I think he's one of the mayor's assistants."

Lauren's brain was racing. She had to find a way to get closer to Detective Dufrene and the others. Then she had an idea.

"Excuse me, Leroy. I need the ladies' room. I'll be right back, and whatever you do, don't let them see you!"

When Lauren returned a few minutes later, Leroy almost didn't recognize her. She was wearing a red dress! A big, black hat was covering her hair, and she wore a pair of oversized sunglasses.

"Where in the world did you..."

"I bought the dress and hat from one of the waitresses," Laura interrupted him. "She was going to wear it to a party after work. Wish me luck. This will be my first undercover job in the 'Big Easy'."

Leroy watched her sway towards Detective Dufrene and the other men. Part of him hoped she knew what she was doing, but the other part was thinking Lauren was very easy on the eyes.

to whisper	flüstern
hang-out	Stammlokal
admission	Eintritt
to sway	schwanken
easy on the eyes	schön anzuschauen, hübsch

Exercise 6: True or false? Welche Aussagen sind korrekt? Markieren Sie mit richtig ✓ oder falsch – !

1. Rene Guidry doesn't have an important position. ❐
2. Leroy has often had romantic relationships with colleagues. ❐
3. There weren't many out of town visitors at Fritzel's. ❐
4. Laura bought other clothes so she could go to a party. ❐

3 Dead Easy

Calliope was eating a late dinner at the police station. Red beans and rice was one of her favorite dishes. The Creole [i] specialty was also cheap, filling and healthy. Calliope asked herself how often during her almost 20 years with the police she had worked late and eaten quickly at her desk or in a police car. Too often, she told herself, and put down her fork. The case she was working on had taken her appetite away, anyway.

Der Begriff **Creole** bezeichnet die Menschen, deren Vorfahren in der Zeit der Kolonialisierung ausgewandert sind. Der Begriff kommt von dem spanischen Verb criar („aufziehen"). Die **Louisiana Creole people** sind also die Nachfahren der Kolonialsiedler in Louisiana, deren Herkunft meist in Frankreich oder Spanien liegt.

She stared at the crime scene photos of the unfortunate Julian Fortune. Somehow, the facts in his murder just didn't make sense. For one thing, he didn't have a police record, and that was strange for a drug dealer. For another, the police had found the drugs and money very easily – too easily. Those journalists turning up at the crime scene were also suspicious. She wished she could talk to somebody else about it. But her partner and most of the other officers she worked with were out on the

Creole	kreolisch
to be out on the town	abends in der Stadt unterwegs sein
nine to five man	jmd., der sich strikt an die geregelten Arbeitszeiten hält
to burn the midnight oil	bis spät in der Nacht arbeiten

town – again. As usual, Clovis hadn't even asked her to go with them.

A knock on the door put an end to her thoughts, and Calliope was surprised to see who it was. Her boss, Commander Bufford Walker, was normally a nine-to-five man.

"Good evening, Detective. Burning the midnight oil, again?"

"Yes, sir. And you, too, I see."

"Well, the mayor's really putting pressure on us to solve the tourist shooting quickly. Is that what's keeping you here so late?"

"No sir, that's not my case. I'm going over the Fortune shooting."

Calliope paused when she saw the Commander's face.

"I believe that one is fairly clear, Detective. But even you are going to have a hard time finding out who shot him."

Calliope wasn't sure if that "even you" was meant as a compliment about her high rate of solving murder cases.

Exercise 7: Comparatives and superlatives. Lesen Sie weiter und schreiben Sie die fehlenden Steigerungsformen in der richtigen Form auf!

bad | young | far | difficult | good | little

Even though Calliope was the **1.** ______ detective in the police department, she was the **2.** ______ praised. Things had indeed been much **3.** ______ for her when she was **4.** ______, but being a black female cop in New Orleans was still one of the **5.** ______

jobs around. And the majority of her male colleagues had

moved **6.** ______ up the career ladder than she

had.

Calliope's male colleagues didn't openly mob her anymore, but she knew she would never be one of the boys. Not that she wanted to be.

"Detective, the reason I'm here is that I'm forming a special task force to investigate the tourist murder, and I want you to lead the team."

"But what about the Fortune shooting?"

"Dufrene can handle it. I need your talents for the tourist case."

"Why, Commander, I don't know what to say!"

"Just tell me you'll take on the job and get it finished quickly. If you do, it could finally mean a promotion for you."

Commander Walker stopped speaking for a second and looked her carefully in the eye.

to be one of the boys	zu der (meist männlichen) Gruppe gehören
task force	*hier*: Spezialeinheit
promotion	Beförderung
Cajun	Cajun
sip	Schlückchen
signature	*hier*: charakteristisch, typisch

"If, that is, you can prove to me that you are a *real* team player," he added softly.

And there it was. The Commander had finally come out and almost said it. By "real team player" he meant she should keep her

mouth shut if she wanted a better job and a higher salary. He was waiting for her answer.
"Thank you, Commander Walker. I'll do my best."
"Good. I'm sure you will. Here's a file with a list of the other team members. Get a meeting organized for first thing in the morning." The Commander left without even wishing her good night.
"Well, *embrasse moi tchew,*" Calliope said the bad words loudly, as soon as she was sure the Commander couldn't hear her. The Cajun[i] expression meant "kiss my ass." Damn it to hell, Calliope thought. What was she going to do now?

Der Begriff **Cajun** bezeichnet die frankophone Bevölkerungsgruppe in Louisiana, deren akadische Vorfahren Mitte des 18. Jahrhunderts aus der ostkanadischen Provinz Acadie vertrieben worden waren.

Exercise 8: Odd one out. Welches Wort ist das „schwarze Schaf"? Unterstreichen Sie!

1. talented gifted qualified skilled
2. promote move-up advance transfer
3. department task force team working group
4. career job profession work

Back at the jazz club, Lauren took another sip of her hurricane. It was the signature cocktail in New Orleans. One of the cops had ordered it for her. It tasted delicious, but was very strong. So far, she hadn't heard anything that could help with the investigation.

But at least Dufrene and Hart hadn't recognized her – yet. All of the cops were very drunk now, especially Officer Hart. So Lauren decided to focus on him.

"Hey, sugar," she called out to him in an exaggerated Southern drawl. "How about another one of these babies for little old me?"

Leon Hart smiled happily at the beautiful lady who had joined their group. It looked like this could be his lucky night!

"Sure, sweetheart. Anything you want."

"Thanks so much," Lauren told Hart when her drink arrived.

"My pleasure, um, sorry, what was your name again?"

"I didn't say. But it's Candy. Candy Marshall. And yours?"

"I'm Leon Hart. Nice to meet you Candy. Cheers."

The two of them made small talk for a few minutes. Lauren's second hurricane was empty in no time, and Hart ordered again.

"Oh Leon, that's kind of you, but these cocktails are expensive."

"Don't worry Candy, I can afford it. I had a very good day."

"Really?" Lauren asked excitedly. Finally something interesting!

"Yeah, let's just say I had a little windfall. Now drink up!"

"Excuse me, Leon. Who's this pretty lady?"

"Hey, R.C. This is Candy. She's in town for her first Mardi Gras. Candy, this is Richard Charles, but everybody calls him R.C. He's the mayor's right-hand man."

"That sounds like a fascinating job," Lauren drawled. "What exactly do you do for him, R.C.?"

drawl	langgezogene Art zu sprechen
windfall	unverhoffter Gewinn
right-hand man	vertrauter Assistent, rechte Hand
to spot sth.	erkennen
fee	Honorar, Preis
to solicit sb.	*hier*: jmd. zu sexuellen Handlungen auffordern
merchandise	Ware

"Well, whatever he needs doing. And what's your line of work?"
"Me? I'm, uh, I work in sales," Lauren said the first thing that came into her head. But when she saw the looks on the two men's faces, she wished she had told them something else, like maybe that she was a lawyer.
"How much?" R.C. asked her with a knowing smile.
"What do you mean?" Lauren asked – as if she couldn't guess.
"Ah, come on, Candy. You don't have to pretend with us. I can spot a call girl a mile away. How much do you charge per hour?"
"Oh no, wait a minute, R.C. I think you misunderstood me. I'm not a ..."
"Never mind. My boss will be happy to pay more than the usual fee for a night with you."

Exercise 9: Simple or continuous. Lesen Sie weiter und setzen Sie die korrekte Verbform in der Vergangenheit ein!

Lauren couldn't believe what **1.** happen ______________.
The mayor's assistant **2.** think ______________ she was a prostitute, and it **3.** sound ______________ like he was soliciting her for his boss. This **4.** become ______________ dangerous.
"First, though," R.C. **5.** continue ______________, "Let me inspect the merchandise."

But just as he was reaching for Lauren's hat and sunglasses, R.C.'s phone rang. He answered immediately, listened for a few moments and said: "Yes sir, right away, sir."
He ended the call and looked at Lauren.
"Sorry, honey, maybe some other time." Then he turned to Leon. "We have to pay up and get out of here, Hart. Tell the others. We've got urgent business to take care of."
Lauren used the opportunity to excuse herself and almost ran past Leroy into the ladies' room. That was close, she thought. Too close. She waited several minutes before going back into the pub. R.C. and the cops were gone - and so was Leroy!

Calliope wasn't the only one pulling an all-nighter. In her office at WNEO, Ava Clark was also still at her desk. She had watched the footage at least ten times before she spotted the tiny detail. It was very blurry and off to Leroy's right, and almost directly across the street from the shooting. The camera bag was probably swinging, Ava thought. That's why Leroy hadn't seen the person running away from the scene. Ava zoomed in and stared in amazement. The face wasn't completely sharp, but Ava knew who it was. She leaned back in her chair and thought for a few moments. This was big; too big for her, Leroy, and Lauren to handle alone. She picked up the phone to call a friend. Winston Moore was an FBI agent assigned to the Bureau's New Orleans Field Office. Ava and Winston had gone out a few times several years ago. It hadn't

to pull an all-nighter	die Nacht durchmachen
blurry	verschwommen, unscharf
amazement	Erstaunen
demanding	anstrengend, anspruchsvoll
for old times' sake	um der alten Zeiten willen
afterthought	nachträgliche Idee
to yawn	gähnen

worked out. Both of them had demanding careers that hadn't left much time for a relationship. They still kept in touch, though, and Ava was hoping Winston would agree to help her, for old times' sake. But he wasn't answering, and Ava didn't want to leave a message. Quickly, she wrote him a short email addressed to his private account. It was risky, but as an afterthought she attached the footage and added the line "Do you see who I see?" Then, before she could change her mind, she hit the send button and hoped for the best. Ava ejected the memory card, then stretched and yawned as she got up from her chair. It was way past time go home, not that anyone was waiting for her. That made her think of Winston again and she wished she could see his face when he got her email.

Exercise 10: Quiz. Übersetzen Sie die gesuchten Begriffe und enträtseln Sie das Lösungswort!

1. Beförderung □ _ _ _ _ _ _ _ _
2. Ware _ _ □ _ _ _ _ _ _ _ _
3. erkennen _ _ □ _
4. unverhoffter Gewinn _ _ _ □ _ _ _ _
5. Drogen _ _ □ _ _
6. kreolisch □ _ _ _ _ _
7. Spezialeinheit _ _ _ _ _ _ _ _ □
8. Prost _ _ _ _ □ _

Lösung: _ _ _ _ _ _ _ _

Ava walked over to the safe and started to enter the combination. Her back was to the door, so she didn't see it opening. The person who came in also made no sound. Ava didn't even have time to scream. The intruder had their hands around her neck before she even knew what was happening. Strangling her was dead easy. When it was over, the murderer picked up the memory card that had fallen from Ava's hand and hurried to finish the rest of the brutal assignment.

intruder	Eindringling
dead easy	kinderleicht

4 Easy Money

Leroy was following the police officers and the mayor's assistant down Bourbon Street at a safe distance. He was lucky that the Quarter was so full of people celebrating Carnival. It was a pity he didn't have his camera with him. If something worth filming happened, he'd have to make do with the one on his phone. He decided to take it out of his pocket to be ready, just in case. And he should probably call Lauren - she had no idea where he was, or what he was up to. He tried to keep his eyes on the guys in front of him while he found Lauren's number and made the call. When she answered, he quickly explained what he was doing.

to make do with sth.	mit etw. auskommen
just in case	für alle Fälle
to be up to sth.	etw. im Schilde führen

"Lauren I have to go, they're turning down St. Peter Street now. Maybe they're headed for Jackson Square or the riverfront."
"Leroy, please be careful," Lauren managed to say before he hung up on her. "Even I know those places aren't safe at night."
Leroy knew she was right. There were much fewer people and almost no traffic on the street now. The men ahead reached Jackson Square and kept walking, but not as fast now. One of them turned around and almost saw Leroy. Just in time, Leroy was able to jump behind one of the many trees bordering the Square. He switched on the phone's camera and started walking again from tree to tree. But that was stupid because they were blocking his

and the camera's view. Leroy took a deep breath and decided to take a chance. He ducked down and crawled closer. Then he saw headlights coming down the street – slowly. They belonged to a dark SUV with tinted windows.

Exercise 11: Passive Tense. Lesen Sie weiter und ergänzen Sie die fehlenden Verbformen im Passiv!

hide | hand | put down | signal | say | position

The car stopped by the cops and a window 1. ________. A hand came out and Detective Dufrene and the man from the mayor's office 2. ________ to come over. Leroy 3. ________ from view but the camera 4. ________ outside of the trees and aimed towards the car. Leroy couldn't hear what 5. ________, but a few seconds later, Dufrene 6. ________ a large envelope, and the car raced away with squealing tires.

Leroy turned the camera around and prayed he had got the license number. Dufrene was laughing loudly now, so Leroy got the camera pointed back towards him. He was just in time. Dufrene opened the envelope and glanced inside. He quickly took a look around to make sure the group was alone before he pulled out a huge stack of cash. He counted it, then gave each man a share.

"Here you are: your next installment of easy money for work *not* well done."
He laughed again at his own play on words.
"You're a fool, Dufrene," R.C. told him coldly. "Keep your mouth shut and let's get out of here. The mayor's waiting for an easy woman, and I need a drink. Maybe Candy is still at Fritzel's."

Leroy quickly pulled his phone out of sight and held his breath while the men walked past. When he couldn't hear their footsteps anymore, he called Lauren.
"Where are you?" he whispered.
"I'm still at the pub. And you?"
"On my way to the car. Listen, Lauren, the men are coming back to the pub, so get out of there fast. Meet me at the garage!"
Lauren didn't ask any of the million questions she had, but quickly followed Leroy's instructions. A few minutes later she was at the garage and was relieved to see Leroy was already there.
"Oh, Leroy, thank goodness you're safe. I was so worried! How could you have gone off on your own like that?"
"Lauren, there's no time for that now. We need to go back to the station on the double. I think… I hope I have the proof we need for our story. I'll tell you on the way."
When Leroy and Lauren pulled into the station parking lot, they were surprised but glad to see Ava's car in her reserved spot.
The two of them checked in with the night security guard and went directly to her office. Leroy was so excited that he didn't

to duck down	sich bücken
tinted	getönt
to squeal	*hier*: quietschen
to glance	flüchtig blicken
easy money	leicht verdientes Geld
⚡ easy woman	leichtes Mädchen

even bother knocking, but rushed right in. Lauren was right behind him, and the sight that met their eyes was so shocking that it made both of them cry out. Ava Clark's body was hanging from a rope from the ceiling. A chair was turned over on the floor beneath her feet.

At his home in NOLA's Garden District, Agent Wilson Moore was amazed when he saw Ava's email and the attachment. He wondered how in the world she had got hold of this story – and the footage. She had been sketchy about the details, and he suspected it wouldn't be easy getting more information out of her. It was critical for his own investigation, though, so he had to try. Even though it was already after 1:00 a.m., Wilson decided to call her right away. He remembered that Ava had always been a night owl; it was one of the many differences between them. When she didn't pick up at her home number, he tried her on her cell. Wilson tapped his fingers impatiently against his lips and read the email again while he waited for her to pick up.

to rush in	hineinstürzen
to get hold of sth.	*hier*: etw. ergattern, auftreiben
night owl	Nachtmensch
jazz funeral	Jazz-Beerdigung

Ein **Jazz-Funeral** ist ein musikalischer Bestattungsritus, der seinen Ursprung in spirituellen afrikanischen Bräuchen hat.

Leroy and Lauren were still staring in shock at Ava's body when they heard the ringtone coming from the handbag on her desk. It was the melody of "When the Saints Go Marching In," a famous song, often played at jazz funerals in New Orleans. The sound of it was horribly macabre and brought tears to Lauren's eyes.

Exercise 12: Unscramble. **Bringen Sie die Wörter in Avas E-Mail an Agent Wilson in die richtige Reihenfolge!**

1. a police you about of I am WNEO the investigation writing

____

______________________________.

2. shot afternoon our was this killed informant mysteriously and

____

______________________________.

3. what version buy of we police happened the don't

____

______________________________.

4. talk soon about each this see can other to about we

____

______________________________?

5. help can old you for , Ava

hoping sake me times'

____

____.

"Should we answer it, Leroy?" she asked in a shaky voice.
"I don't know. But I can't stand hearing that song just now. I'll do it."
Leroy took out a handkerchief from his pocket and used it to take the phone out of Ava's bag. Before he answered the call, Leroy glanced at the display. It read "Wilson M., FBI, private number."
"Lauren, it's somebody from the FBI calling!" he whispered before he hit the answer key. He waited before saying anything.
"Ava? Are you there?" said the voice on the other end.
"No," Leroy managed to get out. "Leroy Harris speaking."
"This is an old friend of Ava's, Wilson Moore. Can I speak to her, please? It's urgent."
"I'm…I'm sorry Mr. Moore, but something terrible has happened. Ava…Ava's dead. We just found her. I think she killed herself."
Then Leroy, the hardened professional, lost control and broke down in tears. Lauren pulled herself together and took the phone from him.
"This is Lauren LeBlanc. I'm…we're sorry to have to tell you such terrible news, Mr. Moore."
Wilson was speechless. Ava and suicide? No way, he thought. Not in a million years – and especially not when she was working on such a hot story. His own eyes were burning with tears, but he rubbed them away and tried to concentrate.

"It's Agent Moore, Ms. Leblanc. Now tell me quickly where you are and what's going on."

Lauren took a deep breath to steady her nerves and told Agent Moore about how they had found Ava. She didn't tell him about their investigation, though.

"All right. I'll be there as soon as I can. Try and stay calm and please wait right outside Ava's office door. Don't let anyone else inside, and don't touch anything or tell anyone else."

"Agent Moore, I don't know exactly how to put this, but how do we know we can trust you?"

"You can't know, Ms. LeBlanc. But Ava trusted me enough to contact me and outline what she – and you – are working on."

Lauren thought about that for a moment and decided she and Leroy didn't have much choice.

After all, what else could they do? Calling the police wasn't an option.

"All right. I'll inform security to let you in and bring you here."

"Good. But let the guard know I won't be alone, and don't let on that I'm from the FBI."

handkerchief	Taschentuch
to pull oneself together	sich zusammenreißen
suicide	Selbstmord
to steady	*hier*: beruhigen
to let on	durchblicken lassen
briefcase	Aktenkoffer
to let by	vorbei lassen
grim	düster, grimmig

Agent Moore and three FBI forensic experts carrying oversized briefcases reached the station only half an hour later. No one said anything until the guard had left. Then Agent Moore and his team put on gloves and thin plastic covers over their shoes, before he opened the door and let the experts by.

"You two wait here," Agent Moore ordered, before going inside.

He came back out ten minutes later. His face looked grim.

"Is there a place close by where we can talk in private?"

"We can use my office," Lauren offered.

"No, not a good idea," Moore told her. "I'll tell you why later."

"Then let's use the break room," Leroy suggested.

When all three of them were seated around the break room table, Agent Moore started to brief the journalists.

to brief sb.	jmd. kurz informieren
bug	Wanze
to break in	einbrechen

Exercise 13: Fill in the blanks. Lesen Sie weiter und ergänzen Sie mit den passenden Satzteilen!

what's more | additionally | let me start | even though | for one thing

" **1.** ______ by telling you that Ava definitely didn't kill herself. She was murdered! **2.** ______, I think it was an inside job."

3. ______ they were shocked, Lauren and Leroy kept quiet.

" **4.** ______, the marks on her neck don't match the rope. **5.** ______, we found signs of a bug on the ceiling.

"However, what really makes me suspect an insider is that the visitor's sign-in sheet is empty for tonight – except for me and my team."

"But someone could have broken in," Lauren pointed out.

"No, because, finally, you should have a look at these."

5 Getting Off Easy

Lauren and Leroy stared at the photos Agent Moore had put on the table. One showed WNEO's star crime reporter, Vincent Mercier, at a party. In one, he was kissing a beautiful Creole woman. In another, his head was bent over a small mirror with two lines of white powder on it.

"So Vincent's a cokehead?" Lauren said. "But that doesn't prove he killed Ava." To her surprise, Leroy spoke next.

"No, but the woman he's kissing is Julian's half-sister, Celeste. They have, or rather had, the same mother. She died of an overdose when they were children. Julian and Celeste grew up with their drug-dealing uncle." Leroy pointed to a man in another one of the photos. "Him," he added angrily.

to infiltrate	einschleusen
ϟ the Feds	FBI (Spitzname)
curtly	barsch
strictly confidential	streng vertraulich
handy	nützlich
daring	gewagt

"That's Raimond Monery," Agent Moore told Lauren. "The FBI believes he's the most powerful and richest gang boss in NOLA. We've been trying to infiltrate his organization for two years now."

Leroy let out a slow, sad breath. "Then Julian worked for you."

"No. He wouldn't help us because he was too afraid of what Monery might do to his sister. She's an addict, too. Julian wanted to help Celeste, and perhaps he thought working through the media was safer than going undercover with the Feds."

"Well, he was wrong about that," Leroy replied bitterly.

"But who took these pictures, then?" Lauren asked. Then she saw the answer herself in a blurry photo of Monery and two other men. One of them was Leon Hart and Lauren thought she recognized the other man, too. She had seen his photo in the news last night. "That's the man that was shot in the French Quarter yesterday! But he wasn't an ordinary tourist, was he?"

"No," Agent Moore answered curtly. "Giles Dawson was one of our agents working to uncover corruption in the police department. I can't tell you any more now, and the information is strictly confidential. Until, that is, we catch the bad guys."

"Maybe we can help," Leroy offered. Then he finally showed Lauren and Agent Moore the footage on his cell phone and Lauren quickly shared what she had learned at the bar. Her news about the mayor's taste for prostitutes would be especially handy later. The daring plan they came up with had all of them smiling.

"Ava would love this," Leroy said excitedly.

Exercise 14: Between the lines. **Lesen Sie „zwischen den Zeilen" und beantworten Sie die Fragen zum Text in ganzen Sätzen!**

1. Why did Julian inform Leroy and not the Feds?

____

______________________________.

2. Why is the FBI investigating Raimond Monery?

____

______________________________.

3. Why did Julian Harris hate drugs?

____

____.

4. What do the photos of Vincent Mercier prove?

____

____.

Early the next morning, Calliope sat at her kitchen table making plans of her own. She wasn't smiling, though. On the contrary, what she was about to do could cost her everything, including her life. She knew the last cop who had tried to be a whistle-blower had been shot the very same day – supposedly in the line of duty. But Calliope knew better. Every NOLA cop did, and the ones not actively involved in taking kickbacks – or worse – kept quiet out of fear. She looked at the six names on the supposed "task force," and finally laughed out loud. It was a bitter laugh, though. Every name on the list was that of a crooked cop and if she was brave enough, Calliope could prove it.

She had kept careful notes over the years of every criminal act she'd seen a fellow officer commit. With them, she could take down her Commander, too. On the other hand, she could use the notes to "convince" her Commander to give her a promotion and a big raise. The sound of coughing from her son's room helped her to make up her mind. If I don't finally do the right thing, she thought, I'll never be able to look him in the eyes again. Her son, Adam, was 26. Eight years ago, he had been innocently walking down the street when he got caught in the middle of a gang shooting. A bullet had hit Adam in the back and left him paralyzed. The shooter was a member of Raimond Monery's gang, but he had got off easy. Because Monery had friends in high places, Calliope reminded herself. But not much longer, she promised as she took out a business card and looked at the number. She was ready to make the call, but not from home. She would use a payphone.

on the contrary	im Gegenteil
in the line of duty	im Einsatz
crooked	*hier*: betrügerisch
to take down sb.	jmd. zu Fall bringen
paralyzed	gelähmt
to get off easy	leicht davon kommen
friends in high places	einflussreiche Freunde
the powers that be	die Mächtigen

Vincent Mercier was sweating heavily when he got to work the next morning. There hadn't been a story online or in the radio about the death of a WNEO producer. Maybe the powers that be want to keep it quiet, he thought, and reminded himself to look shocked and sad at whoever told him the news.

Exercise 15: Adjective or adverb? Lesen Sie weiter, übersetzen Sie die Ausdrücke und fügen Sie sie richtig ein!

gewöhnlich | glücklich | allzu | misstrauisch | höflich | üblicherweise

But the **1.** ______________ talkative receptionist at the front desk only said good morning **2.** ______________, and didn't mention Ava. In the newsroom, it was also business as **3.** ________________ He saw the new girl laughing **4.** ________________ with Leroy Harris, and Vincent gave her a **5.** ________________ look. He was certain that Lauren was **6.** ________________ ambitious and wanted nothing more than to have his job.

He hated her and wished again that he'd been ordered to kill Lauren instead of Ava, but maybe next time. It looked like no one had found the producer's body yet, which was strange.

"Morning Lauren, Leroy," he said with a fake smile. "Is Ava in her office? I've got a hot tip on the tourist shooting."

"Good morning, Vincent," Lauren answered sweetly. "That's great news about your tip, but I'm afraid you can't talk to Ava about it. She's, Ava's..." Lauren stopped speaking and looked at the floor.

"She's what, Lauren?" Vincent said nicely, but inside he was thinking: thank goodness – now say the words, bitch.

Lauren made him sweat a few more seconds.

"Ava's not coming in today. She called in sick."

"What!" Vincent couldn't help shouting out the word, but quickly got himself under control. "I mean, Ava's never ill."

"Well, she is today. I think she said she has a, um, sore throat."

Vincent tried to look calm, but his face had turned almost white and his heart was beating twice as fast as normal. He made some excuse and walked as fast as he could to his office and slammed the door behind him. Was it possible that Ava had only been unconscious – or even worse, pretended to be dead? That was the only explanation Vincent could think of, and if it was true, he was in serious trouble. Vincent took out a cell phone hidden in his briefcase. Normally, Raimond called him, but Vincent couldn't wait. He wished he could have a quick hit first, but the only rule Vincent still followed was no drugs on the job.

The phone rang ten times before the gang boss picked up.

ambitious	ehrgeizig
ϟ bitch	Miststück
to make sb. sweat	jmd. ins Schwitzen bringen, warten lassen
to slam	zuknallen
ϟ hit	*hier*: Drogen nehmen
to cut sb. off	jmd. unterbrechen
ϟ to take care of sb.	*hier*: jmd. erledigen, töten
ϟ Spit it out!	Raus mit der Sprache!

"This had better be good," Raimond Monery said sleepily. "You woke me up."

"Raimond! Something bad..."

"Shut up, fool!" Raimond cut him off. "No names on the phone."

Shit, Vincent thought. I've already made him angry.

"Sorry, um, sir. It's just I have, well, bad news. The person I took care of last night, there's a problem." Vincent couldn't say it.

"What kind of problem, news guy?"

"It looks like she may not be taken care of."

"What the hell does that mean? You already gave me the card. Did she have something else?"

"I don't know. But I think, it looks like..."

"Just spit it out. I don't have all day."

"No one here is talking about Ava being dead, and someone even said she called in sick this morning."

There was a moment of silence on the other end of the line, but when Raimond Monery spoke again, Vincent turned even paler. "For the last time, you idiot. No names on the phone. Come to our usual meeting place – now."
Then he hung up.

"Gotcha," Agent Moore said softly when he heard the phone call end. It wasn't all that he'd hoped for, but it was good enough. "We have Mr. Vincent Mercier right where we want him," Moore told his team sitting outside the station in the plain FBI van.
"Now, let's go inside and tell him about his career change from star reporter to star witness in our case."
"Are you going to put a bug on him for the meeting with Monery?" asked a younger agent.
It was very tempting, but Agent Moore shook his head no.
"If we let him meet with Raimond, Mercier's a dead man. Besides, Monery is being arrested even as we speak."
Just then, Agent Moore's phone rang. He didn't recognize the number, and he didn't have time to take the call. Vincent Mercier was waiting.
The agents assigned to arrest Raimond Monery were surprised to see him smiling and waiting outside his luxurious home. As they took him away, none of them saw the woman with the bruised face and bleeding lips making phone calls from inside. Julian's sister, Celeste, was following the orders

pale	bleich
↯ gotcha (got you)	Hab ich dich erwischt!
tempting	verlockend, verführerisch
to arrest sb.	jmd. festnehmen
bruised	geprellt
to break sth.	*hier*: eine Nachricht als erster bekannt machen
wide-spread	weit verbreitet
to roll	*hier*: laufen (Kamera, Film)

Exercise 16: Other meanings. Finden Sie Ausdrücke im Text, die auch folgende Bedeutungen haben können!

1. remove ______________________
2. to look after ______________________
3. to expectorate ______________________
4. strike ______________________

her uncle had beaten into her. She had learned the hard way that it didn't pay to disobey.

Outside the television station, Lauren was giving a live report. She had convinced her boss that the story about Vincent was too big to keep quiet. It was better if WNEO broke it themselves, or as much of it as possible until Agent Moore let them tell the rest.

"Many details remain unknown," Lauren spoke into the camera Leroy was holding. "But what we do know is that the FBI has arrested WNEO's star crime reporter, Vincent Mercier, for the murder of our producer, Ava Clarke. Mercier is also being questioned about numerous other crimes, including drug and gang activity and," Lauren paused for a moment, "wide-spread corruption in the New Orleans' Police Department."

Lauren introduced the footage Leroy had taken at Julian's shooting. As it rolled, she described her and Leroy's own investigation. The video froze on the face of a man running away from the crime scene. It was Officer Leon Hart. Just as Lauren began to explain its importance, she saw Leroy point behind her.

"We'll return to that part of the story in a moment. Right now, Mr. Mercier is being led from the television station in handcuffs."

Vincent still couldn't grasp what was happening to him. He should be the one going live, reporting on a criminal. The thought made him look directly into Leroy's camera. He was still staring into it when the shots rang out.
One of the bullets from Leon Hart's gun slammed into Vincent's chest and almost knocked him down. The second went through his head. Celeste had followed orders and so had Leon. After all, what was one more shooting in "The City that Care Forgot"? Then he did the rest of the job and put down his gun and raised his hands in the air. Now Leon just had to keep quiet until Raimond's hotshot lawyer arrived and then stick to the deal. Leon would be the scapegoat, and his friends in high places would get him an easy time in prison and a whole lot of money when he got out.

to grasp sth.	etw. begreifen
hotshot	*hier*: Star
scapegoat	Sündenbock
to slap	klatschen

Calliope listened to the sound of the phone ringing and ringing. She was standing at an open phone booth in a quiet side street not too far from work. It was the third one she'd used in the past hour trying to reach Agent Moore.
"Why doesn't he pick up?"
She didn't realize she had spoken out loud until her partner's voice whispered in her ear.
"Because he's busy, Cal."
Then Calliope felt Dufrene's gun pressing into her back and started to scream. Her partner slapped a hand over her mouth.
"You don't want to do that, Cal," he told her softly. "Think of your son and come with me. The Commander wants to talk to you. Just remember, murder's made easy here – almost as easy as the city itself."

Final Test

Solutions

Glossary

List of Exercises

Final Test

Exercise 1: Presentation Notes. **Vervollständigen Sie PSO Wilsons Notizen für das Meeting!**

1. V _ _ _ _ _ _ : Miquel Alvarado, Candace Green.
2. S _ _ _ _ _ _ _ : Sophie Martin-Woods, Rosa? Others?
3. M _ _ _ _ : bomb in f _ _ _ _ _ _ _ _ _ ,
   d _ _ _ _ _ _ _ _ with smart phone.
4. B _ _ _ _ _ _ _ _ _ : remind all to say anything that
   p _ _ _ into their h _ _ _ _ !

Exercise 2: Idiomatic Expressions. **Vervollständigen Sie die Sätze aus „Manhattan Murder“!**

1. She is happy to teach him her tricks of the ________________.

   a) knowledge **b)** shop **c)** trade **d)** occasion

2. The identity of a witness can really make or

_______________ a case.

a) take b) break c) ache d) stake

3. The culprit has already _______________ town.

a) skipped b) jumped c) hopped d) spun

4. I have lost _______________ of my husbands whereabouts.

a) position b) around c) track d) hope

5. Ted received a call from the property clerk that

_______________ the case in motion.

a) put b) set c) kept d) brought

6. For a moment, he is _______________ for words.

a) lost b) gone c) looking d) empty

Exercise 3: Who is who? Ordnen sie die Charaktere aus „Murder Made Easy" der passenden Beschreibung zu!

1. ☐ Lauren LeBlanc a) has a senior position
2. ☐ Leon Hart b) was killed in the line of duty
3. ☐ Calliope Carollo c) is a rookie
4. ☐ Giles Dawson d) is a moonlighter

Exercise 4: Crossword puzzle. **Finden Sie die gesuchten Begriffe aus „Manhattan Murder“ und lösen Sie das Kreuzworträtsel!**

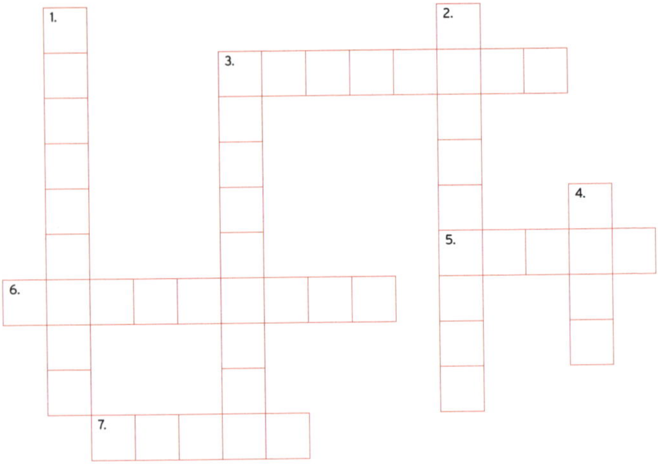

Across

3. proof

5. to reprimand

6. to expand on

7. a turn (in a story)

Down

1. at first

2. never stopping

3. to shame

4. to make a request

Exercise 5: Unscramble the sentences. **Bringen Sie die Wörter in die richtige Reihenfolge und bilden Sie sinnvolle Sätze!**

1. murderous | of | boss | in | Nathan's | charge | netowrk | is | the

____

____.

2. was | farm | and | Miguel | vandalized | was | his | organic | threatened

____

____.

3. urban | his | cash | want | Miguel | didn't | out | farm | want | to

____

____.

4. change | the | Wilson | about | made | think | case | career | a | about

____

____.

Exercise 6: Match up. Verbinden Sie die Personen aus „Manhattan Murder" mit ihren Gewohnheiten!

1. loves hamburgers	a) Mekko Harjo
2. lives in New Jersey	b) Emily Peters
3. studied photography	c) Richie Halter
4. wears a baseball cap	d) Maria Esteves
5. works for the Properties Bureau	e) Ricky Gluski

Exercise 7: Idioms. Ordnen Sie die Redewendungen aus „Murderous Network" ihren Definitionen zu!

1. ☐ to be right on the money	a) suddenly understand
2. ☐ to save one's breath	b) start over
3. ☐ to go back to the drawing board	c) not worth getting upset
4. ☐ to hit home	d) on target

Exercise 8: Translate. Finden Sie die Übersetzung der folgenden Wörter aus allen drei Kurzkrimis!

1. nachdenklich ____________	3. Verwarnung ____________
2. geprellt ____________	4. Informant ____________

Exercise 9: Passive to active. **Wandeln Sie die folgenden Passivsätze in Aktivsätze um!**

1. Leon hopes he will be given an easy time by his friends in high places.

   ____

   ______________________________.

2. Lauren was assigned to an undercover investigation by Ava.

   ____

   ______________________________.

3. Some NOLA cops are being given kickbacks from gangs.

   ____

   ______________________________.

4. Calliope had been mobbed by other police officers.

   ____

   ______________________________.

Solutions

Murderous Network

Exercise 1: **1.** want **2.** fight **3.** ask **4.** work **5.** homework

Exercise 2: **1.** off **2.** away **3.** in **4.** on **5.** over **6.** of

Exercise 3: **1.** b **2.** d **3.** a **4.** c

Exercise 4: **1.** Accept (Except) **2.** talk (say) **3.** meaning (opinion) **4.** personnel (personal) **5.** make (do) **6.** long (late)

Exercise 5: **1.** c **2.** a **3.** b **4.** a

Exercise 6: **1.** false (The profit was $ 1000.) **2.** false (His father wants him to stay on the farm.) **3.** true **4.** false (She had been at a reception for investors.)

Exercise 7: **1.** entered **2.** were crying **3.** was sitting **4.** had **5.** was holding

Exercise 8: **1.** gone over the edge **2.** to make a split-second decision **3.** alternative **4.** evidence

Exercise 9: **1.** a supervisor **2.** an Assistant Chief **3.** a trainee **4.** a higher-up

Exercise 10: **1.** overtime **2.** paid off **3.** information **4.** desk **5.** presentation **6.** session

Exercise 11: **1.** Give a short update about what we have learnt so far. **2.** Discuss things we do not know. **3.** Hold a team brainstorming session about unknown factors. **4.** Ask for questions and give instructions about our next steps.

Exercise 12: **1.** lump sum **2.** suicide **3.** shares **4.** lead

Exercise 13:

I	G	R	B	O	I	L	N	S	A
A	C	C	O	U	N	T	L	I	X
M	B	S	U	E	V	A	E	L	K
I	N	C	O	M	E	P	G	O	F
U	C	D	Q	U	S	E	A	L	I
M	A	R	K	E	T	W	C	C	N
O	S	B	Y	R	M	H	Y	S	A
L	H	U	A	W	E	I	M	R	N
T	A	Y	N	U	N	E	S	U	C
P	R	O	F	I	T	A	B	L	E
B	I	U	K	Y	C	R	S	M	E
L	D	T	U	R	N	O	V	E	R

Exercise 14: **1.** didn't sleep **2.** fought **3.** stole **4.** made **5.** drank **6.** sent

Exercise 15: **1.** had made **2.** had done **3.** to make **4.** to do **5.** did **6.** making

Exercise 16: **1.** a professional development course **2.** thinking outside of the box **3.** sign off on it **4.** eye to eye.

Manhattan Murder

Exercise 1: **1.** destination **2.** appear **3.** promote **4.** schedule

Exercise 2: **1.** with **2.** by **3.** of **4.** to **5.** of **6.** until

Exercise 3: **1.** His building aggression for the moment vanishes. **2.** I do not know what to tell you. **3.** We found a note in her pocket. **4.** The quickest way across the river is by ferry.

Exercise 4: **1.** Did **2.** shook **3.** got **4.** was **5.** saw **6.** wore **7.** nodded **8.** said

Exercise 5: **1.** b **2.** d **3.** a **4.** c

Exercise 6: **1.** false (It is Ted's first week.) **2.** false (They are very friendly.) **3.** true **4.** false (He went to see Marjorie's family.) **5.** true **6.** false (She is Ted's wife.)

Exercise 7: **1.** b **2.** e **3.** d **4.** a **5.** C

Exercise 8: **1.** an **2.** the **3.** a **4.** blank **5.** the **6.** the **7.** blank

Exercise 9: **1.** ask **2.** reservoir **3.** pretty **4.** Excitement

Exercise 10: **1.** a **2.** b **3.** a **4.** a

Exercise 11: **1.** By **2.** from **3.** between **4.** to **5.** over **6.** With

Exercise 12: **1.** Ted points to the left side of the certificate. **2.** Emily walks over and pulls a document out of the file. **3.** What other man would want to kill Marjorie? **4.** Ted can suddenly hear her deep and raspy southern drawl.

Exercise 13: **1.** the (his) **2.** about (on) **3.** passed (past) **4.** became (becomes) **5.** their (they're) **6.** off (of)

Exercise 14: **1.** c **2.** e **3.** f **4.** b **5.** d **6.** a

Exercise 15: **1.** As Ted and Emily were driving, their sirens were sounding. **2.** The sun was setting and the maids were lighting the candles. **3.** Mekko was feeling a sudden dread. **4.** I was looking forward to my second.

Murder Made Easy

Exercise 1: **1.** d, h **2.** c, e **3.** a, f **4.** b, g

Exercise 2: **1.** do **2.** was **3.** did **4.** is **5.** have

Exercise 3: **1.** moonlight **2.** transfer **3.** SOPs **4.** reprimand

Exercise 4: **1.** office **2.** hair **3.** desk **4.** volume **5.** watching

Exercise 5: **1.** to call it a night **2.** to come clean **3.** to praise **4.** to turn a blind eye to

Exercise 6: **1.** false (He is the Mayor, a "really big fish".) **2.** false (It was his policy not to get involved with women at work.) **3.** true (Fritzel's was not touristy.) **4.** false (She bought them to go undercover.)

Exercise 7: **1.** best **2.** least **3.** worse **4.** younger **5.** most difficult **6.** further/farther

Exercise 8: **1.** qualified **2.** transfer **3.** department **4.** work

Exercise 9: **1.** was happening **2.** thought **3.** sounded **4.** was becoming **5.** continued

Exercise 10: **1.** promotion **2.** merchandise **3.** spot **4.** windfall **5.** drugs **6.** Creole **7.** task force **8.** cheers **Lösung:** producer

Exercise 11: **1.** was put down **2.** were signalled **3.** was hidden **4.** was positioned **5.** was being said **6.** was handed

Exercise 12: **1.** I'm writing you about a WNEO investigation of the police. **2.** Our informant was mysteriously shot and killed this afternoon. **3.** We don't buy the police version of what happened. **4.** Can we see each other soon to talk about this?

Exercise 13: **1.** Let me start **2.** what's more **3.** Even though **4.** For one thing **5.** Additionally

Exercise 14: **1.** Julian informed Leroy because they were old friends. He was afraid of what Raimond might do to Celeste if he caught Julian working with the FBI. **2.** The FBI is investigating Raimond Monery because of his gang and drug dealing activities – and also his connection to the police. **3.** Julian hated drugs because his mother died of a drug overdose, his sister is an addict and his uncle is a dealer. **4.** The photos prove that Vincent used cocaine and had contact with Raimond Monery and at least one corrupt police officer (Leon Hart).

Exercise 15: **1.** normally **2.** politely **3.** usual **4.** happily **5.** suspicious **6.** too

Exercise 16: **1.** cut off **2.** take care of **3.** spit out **4.** hit

Final Test

Exercise 1: **1.** victims **2.** suspects **3.** means, fertilizer, detonated **4.** Brainstorm, pops, heads

Exercise 2: **1.** c **2.** b **3.** a **4.** c **5.** b **6.** a

Exercise 3: **1.** c **2.** d **3.** a **4.** b **5.** e

Exercise 4:

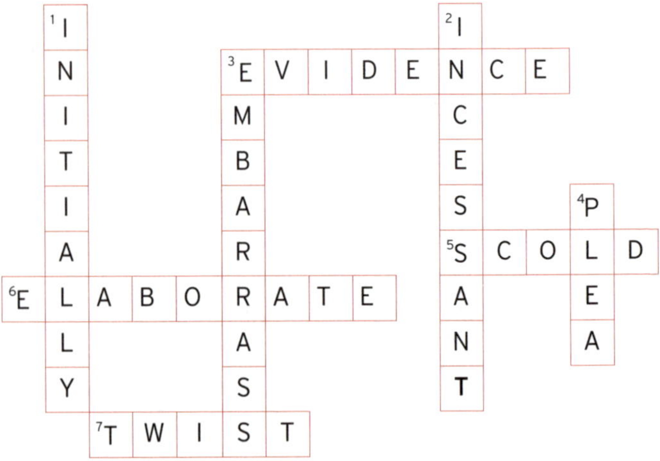

Exercise 5: **1.** Nathan's boss is in charge of the murderous network. **2.** Miguel was threatened and his organic farm was vandalized. **3.** Miguel didn't want to cash out his urban farm. **4.** The case made Wilson think about a career change.

Exercise 6: **1.** e **2.** b **3.** a **4.** d **5.** c

Exercise 7: **1.** d **2.** c **3.** b **4.** a

Exercise 8: **1.** pensively **2.** bruised **3.** reprimand **4.** whistle-blower

Exercise 9: **1.** Leon hopes his friends in high places will give him easy time. **2.** Ava assigned Lauren to an undercover investigation. **3.** Gangs are giving some NOLA cops kickbacks. **4.** Other police officers had mobbed Calliope.

Glossary

ϟ= umgangssprachlich
pl = Plural

abandoned	ausrangiert; verlassen
absentmindedly	geistesabwesend
according to	laut, gemäß
acre	Hektar
to add one's two cents	seinen Senf dazugeben
admission	Eintritt
to admit	zugeben
affirmatively	zustimmend, bejahend
afterthought	nachträgliche Idee
agitation	Aufregung
ajar	halb offen, angelehnt
amazement	Erstaunen
ambitious	ehrgeizig
appalled	erschrocken, entsetzt
to appear	erscheinen
appointment	Termin
to approach	erreichen, sich nähern
to arrest sb.	jmd. festnehmen
ascent	Aufstieg, Fahrt nach oben
to assign	zuweisen
assignment	Aufgabe
Assistant Chief	Stellvertretender Leiter (Polizei, Feuerwehr)
astonished	erstaunt
attempt	versuchen
to attract	anziehen, reizen

to back out of sth.	aus etw. aussteigen
to bare one's teeth at sb.	jmd. die Zähne zeigen
to be after sth.	hinter etw. her sein
to be caught off guard	überrascht/überrumpelt werden
ϟ to be dying to know sth.	etw. unbedingt wissen wollen
to be on edge	genervt sein
to be on good terms with sb.	mit jmd. auf gutem Fuß stehen
to be one of the boys	zu der (meist männlichen) Gruppe gehören
to be out on the town	abends in der Stadt unterwegs sein
to be right on the money	den Nagel auf den Kopf treffen
to be up to sth.	etw. im Schilde führen
big fish	hohes Tier
ϟ bitch	Miststück
blankly	ausdruckslos
blurry	verschwommen, unscharf
brain child	Idee, Erfindung
to break in	einbrechen
to break sth.	*hier*: eine Nachricht als erster bekannt machen
breathtaking	atemberaubend
to brief sb.	jmd. kurz informieren
briefcase	Aktenkoffer
bright	*hier*: intelligent
bruised	geprellt
bug	Wanze
to burn the midnight oil	bis spät in der Nacht arbeiten
to burp	rülpsen, aufstoßen
to bury	beerdigen
ϟ business is booming	das Geschäft läuft gut
to buy out	eine Abfindung zahlen
Cajun	Cajun
to call it a night	Feierabend machen
to capitulate	aufgeben, sich ergeben
career change	berufliche Neuorientierung
case load	Anzahl der Fälle
to cash out	Vermögen verkaufen
to certify	bescheinigen, zertifizieren

to claim	behaupten
to collapse	zusammenbrechen
to come around	nachgeben, einlenken
to come clean	auspacken
to come forward	*hier*: sich stellen
to comfort	trösten
to command	anordnen, befehlen
to compare	vergleichen
to compile	zusammentragen
complex of buildings	Gebäudekomplex
to conceal	verdecken, kaschieren
to confirm	bestätigen
consider	betrachten
to convince sb.	jmd. überzeugen
coroner	Rechtsmediziner
cozy	gemütlich
Creole	kreolisch
crooked	*hier*: betrügerisch
to curse	fluchen
to cut sb. off	jmd. unterbrechen
curtly	barsch
daring	gewagt
day off	freier Tag
dead easy	kinderleicht
delight	Entzücken
to demand	verlangen
demanding	anstrengend, anspruchsvoll
DMV (Department of Motor Vehicles)	Kraftfahrzeug-Zulassungsstelle
drawl	langgezogene Art zu sprechen
to duck down	sich bücken
easy come, easy go	wie gewonnen, so zerronnen
easy money	leicht verdientes Geld
easy on the eyes	schön anzuschauen, hübsch
ϟ easy woman	leichtes Mädchen
to elaborate	ausführen, ausarbeiten
EMT (Emergency Medical Technician)	Sanitäter

evidence	Beweise, Beweismaterial
to examine	untersuchen
executive	leitende(r) Angestellte(r)
exhausted	erschöpft
to expect	erwarten
faintly	leicht, schwach
family law	Familienrecht
fee	Honorar, Preis
fertilizer	Dünger
finding	Entdeckung
to flip through sth.	etw. durchblättern
to flop down	sich plumpsen lassen
footage	Filmmaterial
to forge	fälschen
for old times' sake	um der alten Zeiten willen
for sth. to pop into one's head	jmd. plötzlich einfallen
frenzy	Rausch
friends in high places	einflussreiche Freunde
funeral	Beerdigung
gambling debts *pl*	Spielschulden
garments *pl*	Kleidung
to gesture towards sth.	auf etw. zeigen
to get going	*hier*: in Fahrt kommen
to get hold of sth.	*hier*: etw. ergattern, auftreiben
to get off easy	leicht davon kommen
to get on sb.'s bad side	sich bei jmd. unbeliebt
to glance	flüchtig blicken
to go back to the drawing board	nochmal von vorne anfangen
ϟ to go over the edge	den Verstand verlieren
gossip	Klatsch, Gerüchte
ϟ gotcha (got you)	Hab ich dich erwischt!
to grab	packen
to grasp at straws	nach jedem Strohhalm greifen
to grasp sth.	*hier*: etw. begreifen
greenhouse	Gewächshaus
to grieve	trauern
grim	düster, grimmig

to grieve	trauern
grim	düster, grimmig
guardian	Vormund
gut instinct	Bauchgefühl
handkerchief	Taschentuch
handy	nützlich
hang-out	Stammlokal
hardened professional	harter Brocken
to have a hard time	Schwierigkeiten haben
to hire sb.	jmd. einstellen, anheuern
headquarters	Firmenhauptsitz
to hesitate	zögern
higher-up	hohes Tier
ϟ to hit	*hier*: Drogen nehmen
ϟ to hit home	ankommen
homicide	Mord
hotshot	*hier*: Star
impatient	ungeduldig
to infiltrate	einschleusen
to inherit	erben
to interrupt sb.	jmd. unterbrechen
in the line of duty	im Einsatz
inheritance	Erbschaft
intercom	Wechselsprechanlage
intern	Praktikant
intruder	Eindringling
irrigation	Bewässerungssystem
jazz funeral	Jazz-Beerdigung
just in case	für alle Fälle
kickbacks *pl*	Bestechungsgelder, Schmiergeld
to kneel	knien
lawn	Rasen
lead	*hier*: Hinweis
legacy	Vermächtnis
to let by	vorbei lassen
to let on	durchblicken lassen
to let sth. drag	etw. ziehen, schleifen lassen
to let sth. go	etw. auf sich beruhen lassen

license	Führerschein
likely	wahrscheinlich
to live up to sth.	etw. gerecht werden
to lose one's temper	die Beherrschung verlieren
to lose track	den Überblick verlieren
lost for words	sprachlos
lump sum	einmaliger Betrag, Pauschale
to lure	locken
to moonlight	nebenbei schwarzarbeiten
to mutter	murren
Madre de Dios (*Spanish*)	Mutter Gottes
to make do with sth.	mit etw. auskommen
to make ends meet	über die Runden kommen
to make or break	entscheidend sein
to make sb. sweat	jmd. ins Schwitzen bringen, warten lassen
to make up for	wieder gut machen
mantelpiece	Kamineinfassung
Mardi Gras (Fat Tuesday)	Faschingsdienstag
marigold	Ringelblume
means *pl*	Mittel, Methode
merchandise	Ware
murder-suicide	Mord mit anschließendem Selbstmord
nastily	auf gemeine Art und Weise
to net	*hier*: etw. einbringen
nickname	Spitzname
night owl	Nachtmensch
nine to five man	jmd., der sich strikt an die geregelten Arbeitszeiten hält
↯ to not want to go there	über etw. nicht sprechen/ nachdenken wollen
to obtain	bekommen, erhalten
on the contrary	im Gegenteil
on the double	sofort
opportunity	Gelegenheit, Möglichkeit
orchard	Obstplantage
organic farming	biologische Landwirtschaft

to overlook	übersehen
pale	bleich
paralyzed	gelähmt
partial match	partielle Übereinstimmung
parties *pl*	*hier*: die Beteiligten
pay check	Gehaltscheck
pensively	nachdenklich
periodically	regelmäßig wiederkehrend
persuasion	Beeinflussung, Überzeugung
pick-your-own	Selbstpflück-
ϟ to play hardball	mit harten Bandagen kämpfen
to play it safe	auf Nummer sicher gehen
plea	Bitte
policy	Grundsätze, Strategie
practically	*hier*: so gut wie
to praise	loben
precinct	*hier*: Polizeirevier
precisely	genau
to pretend	so tun als ob
professional development course	Weiterbildungskurs
to promote sb.	jmd. befördern
promotion	Beförderung
property clerk	Immobilienkaufmann
proud	stolz
to prove	beweisen
PSO (Public Safety Officer)	Sicherheitsbeauftragter
to pull an all-nighter	die Nacht durchmachen
to pull oneself together	sich zusammenreißen
to put sth. on the market	etw. auf den Markt bringen
to race	rennen
rage	Wut
rarely	selten
raspy	heiser, kratzig
real estate	Immobilien
reception	Empfang
receptionist	Rezeptionist
to recognize	erkennen

Compact Lernkrimi
Audio-Learning

Compact Lernkrimi
Sprachkurs

Compact Lernkrimi Audio-Learning	Compact Lernkrimi Sprachkurs	
	Englisch für Anfänger (A1/A2) ISBN 978-3-8174-7784-5	A1
Verschollen im Dartmoor ISBN 978-3-8174-7796-8		A2
Totenstille im Hyde Park ISBN 978-3-8174-7797-5		B1
		B2
		C1/C2